新时代行业英语系列教材

总主编 姜　宏　　　副主编 刘雁琪
主　编 曲琳娜　　　原版作者 Catrin E. Morris

旅游英语
ENGLISH for Tourism

清华大学出版社
北　京

U0360713

北京市版权局著作权合同登记号　图字：01-2021-1544

© licensed by ELI s.r.l, Italy — ELI Publishing.
www.elionline.com
Author: Catrin E. Morris

The English adaptation rights arranged through Rightol Media.（本书英文改编版版权经由锐拓传媒取得）

图书在版编目（CIP）数据

旅游英语 / 姜宏总主编；曲琳娜主编. —北京：清华大学出版社，2021.4（2025.2重印）
新时代行业英语系列教材
ISBN 978-7-302-57798-0

Ⅰ.①旅…　Ⅱ.①姜…　②曲…　Ⅲ.①旅游–英语–高等职业教育–教材　Ⅳ.①F59

中国版本图书馆 CIP 数据核字（2021）第 055423 号

策划编辑：刘细珍
责任编辑：刘细珍
封面设计：子　一
责任校对：王凤芝
责任印制：丛怀宇

出版发行：清华大学出版社
　　　　网　　址：https://www.tup.com.cn, https://www.wqxuetang.com
　　　　地　　址：北京清华大学学研大厦 A 座　　邮　　编：100084
　　　　社 总 机：010-83470000　　　　邮　　购：010-62786544
　　　　投稿与读者服务：010-62776969, c-service@tup.tsinghua.edu.cn
　　　　质 量 反 馈：010-62772015, zhiliang@tup.tsinghua.edu.cn
印 装 者：北京博海升彩色印刷有限公司
经　　销：全国新华书店
开　　本：210mm×285mm　　印　　张：6.75　　　字　　数：161 千字
版　　次：2021 年 4 月第 1 版　　　印　　次：2025 年 2 月第 4 次印刷
定　　价：49.00 元

产品编号：091256-02

在经济全球化和国际交往日益频繁的今天，无论是作为个人还是组织的一员，参与国际交流与合作都需要具备良好的外语沟通能力和扎实的专业技术能力。高等学校承担着培养具有全球竞争力的高端技术人才的使命，需要探索如何有效地培养学生的行业外语能力。行业外语教学一直是学校的短板，缺少合适的教材是其中一个主要原因。目前，国内大多数学校在第一学年开设公共英语课程，所用教材多为通用英语教材，其主题与学生所学专业的关联度总体较低；部分院校自主开发的行业英语教材，在专业内容的系统性、语言表达的准确性等方面存在诸多不足；还有部分院校直接采用国外原版的大学本科或研究生教材，但这些教材学术性和专业性太强，对以就业为导向的学生来说，十分晦涩难懂。

清华大学出版社从欧洲引进原版素材并组织国内一线行业英语教师改编的这套"新时代行业英语系列教材"，以提升学生职业英语能力为目标，服务师生教与学。本套教材具有如下特点：

一、编写理念突出全球化和国际化

本套教材在欧洲原版引进优质资源的基础上改编而成，全球化视角选材，结合行业领域和单元主题，关注环境保护、人口老龄化、贫困等时代难题，培养学生的国际视野和世界公民素养。单元主题、板块编排和练习设计与国际接轨，体现国际规范和国际标准，且反映全球行业发展动态和前景，帮助学生全面了解全球行业现状和掌握国际操作流程，夯实行业知识体系。

二、编写目标注重培养学生使用英语完成工作任务的实际应用能力

为响应外语教学改革号召，培养具有国际竞争力的高端技术人才，将外语教学目标由原来的语言能力导向转变为职业能力导向，本套教材通过听、说、读、写、译等基本语言技能训练，让学生完成不同行业领域的工作任务，将英语放到职场的背景中来学，放到员工的岗位职责、工作流程中来学。

三、结构与内容紧扣行业领域的职场情境和核心业务

本套教材围绕行业核心概念和业务组织教学单元，不同单元相互关联，内容由浅入深、由易到难，循序渐进；教材各单元主题契合行业典型工作场景，内容反映职业岗位核心业务知识与流程。每本教材根据内容设置 8 至 10 个单元，用多种形式的语言训练任务提升学生对行业知识的理解与应用。

四、资源立体多样，方便师生教与学

　　本套教材图文并茂。通过改编，在原版教材基础上每个单元增加了学习目标，明确了学生在完成各单元学习后应该达到的知识和能力水平；增加了重点词汇中文注释和专业术语表，便于学生准确理解行业核心概念；听力练习和阅读篇章均配有音频，并借助二维码扫码听音的形式呈现，实现教材的立体化，方便学生学习；习题安排契合单元的主题内容，便于检测单元学习目标的实现程度。教材另配有电子课件和习题答案，方便教师备课与授课。教师可以征订教材后联系出版社索取。

　　本套教材共10本，包括《护理英语》《机电英语》《建筑工程英语》《运输与物流英语》《烹饪、餐饮与接待英语》《旅游英语》《银行与金融英语》《市场营销与广告英语》《商务英语》《商务会谈英语》，涵盖医药卫生、机电设备、土木建筑、交通运输、旅游、财经商贸等六大类专业。建议各学校结合本校人才培养目标，开设相应课程。

　　本套教材适合作为行业英语教材，也适合相关行业从业人员作为培训或自学教材。

姜宏

2021年3月31日

　　《旅游英语》是根据清华大学出版社从欧洲引进的原版英语教材 *Flash on English for Tourism* 改编出版的行业英语教材。内容设计贴合当代大学生（特别是高职高专在校生）和旅游英语专业学习者的英语听、说、读、写水平和兴趣点，可供广大应用型本科和高职院校旅游英语综合类课程使用。

　　《旅游英语》立足我国当前英语教学实际，在尊重原版教材的基础上，明确课程总体教学目标。基于学习者对旅游英语相关知识的学习需求，着力培养学习者的旅游英语综合应用能力。教材编写遵循旅游行业真实交际场景，解析真实交际方法，帮助学习者掌握常用交际用语，实践真实旅游行业情境任务，以原版丰富、鲜活、地道的教学资源为基础，通过导入、阅读1、听说、阅读2、写作的教学环节设计，将旅游英语训练内容有机组合，环环相扣，科学引导学习者进行有效学习和切实应用。

　　教材选材丰富，涵盖行业整体介绍、旅游商品营销、酒店住宿交通、旅游线路规划、旅游行业口语写作沟通技巧、旅游目的地概况、行业应用文写作等方面，激励学习者探究旅游行业英语特色，激发学习热情和兴趣。练习设计紧扣教材内容和教学目标，针对性极强，教学设计多样化，激发学习者学习积极性。

　　"新时代行业英语系列教材"的总主编为北京财贸职业学院国际教育学院姜宏教授。来自北京财贸职业学院各专业的十几位资深教师参与了该套教材的研发、设计和改编工作。姜宏教授在教材编写过程中给予指导，并负责整套教材的总体规划、思路策划、方案制定、体例统筹和书稿审定。本教材主编曲琳娜负责本教材整体体例设计、内容选定、教学方法设定、编写内容分配等工作，同时负责第一章至第八章教材内容的编写；副主编刘雁琪负责第九章和第十章的编写。

　　在我国高等院校旅游英语教学持续深化改革、砥砺前行、不断奋斗的新时期，本教材的出版可谓"及时雨"。我们希望并相信，本教材将以其够用、实用、适用、好用等鲜明特色，成为旅游英语教学领域的一本经典教材。囿于编者水平，教材中难免有疏误之处，竭诚欢迎专家和读者批评指正。

编者

2021年2月1日

Contents

Unit	Topic	Vocabulary	Skills
6 p. 48	**Written & Oral Communication**	• Emails • Memos and forms • Business letters • Phone calls and voice mails	**Reading:** how to write emails, memos, forms and business letters; how to make a phone call and a voice mail **Listening:** booking a hotel; creating an effective voice mail message **Speaking:** mini-telephone conversations **Writing:** a business letter confirming hotel reservation information
7 p. 60	**International Tourism**	• Natural features • Holiday activities • Expressions for recommending	**Reading:** winter/summer holiday resorts and itineraries in Europe; profile on India **Listening and Speaking:** making plans for holiday destinations and activities; booking sightseeing trips **Writing:** a "Must Do" guide
8 p. 70	**Ecotourism**	• History and principles of ecotourism • Organisations involved • Travel habits	**Reading:** ecotourism projects; identifying principles and benefits **Listening:** a radio interview about new holiday destinations **Speaking:** planning sports tourism itineraries **Writing:** an email giving information about ecotourism holidays
9 p. 80	**New Tourist Destinations**	• Sporting events • Types of tourists • Dates and competitions	**Reading:** articles about new tourist destinations and sports tourism **Listening and Speaking:** presenting new tourist destination projects and answering questions about them **Writing:** a plan for new tourist destinations and activities
10 p. 90	**Applying for a Job**	• Curriculum Vitae • Covering letter • Tips for a successful interview	**Reading:** how to write a CV and a covering letter **Listening:** describing what a position involves **Speaking:** discussing the suitability of a candidate compared with a job post; simulating an interview **Writing:** production of a covering letter and CV

UNIT 1

An Introduction to Travel and Tourism

Learning Objectives

Upon completion of the unit, students should be able to:

- understand the basic concepts and latest development of the tourism industry;
- apply the vocabulary on travel and tourism;
- communicate with travel agency about types of holiday;
- explain online operation of travel and tourism services.

Starting Off

1 **Look at the pictures and answer the questions.**

1) Do these people travel?

2) Are they tourists?

3) When and why would you like to travel?

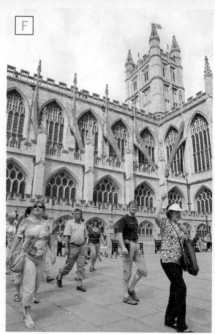

Reading 1

People travel for lots of reasons. They make **journeys** to and from school or work every day; visit friends and family; take day trips shopping or to football **matches**; go out for evening entertainment such as the cinema; and they go away on business or study trips. So when does travel become tourism? When people travel to and stay in a place which is not where they live. For example there is **recreational** tourism if you want to relax and have fun, maybe at the beach. There's **cultural** tourism: **sightseeing** or visiting museums to learn about history, art and people's lifestyles. With **adventure** tourism you **explore distant** places or do **extreme** activities. **Ecotourism** is about **ethical** and responsible trips to natural environments such as **rainforests**. Winter tourism is usually holidays in **resorts** where there is snow and people go skiing or snowboarding. Sport tourism is to play or watch different sporting events like the Olympics. Educational tourism is to learn something, possibly a foreign language, abroad. Nowadays there is also health tourism to look after your body and mind by visiting places like spa resorts; **religious** tourism to celebrate religious events or visit important religious places such as **Mecca** for **Muslims**; and **gap-year** tourism when young people **go backpacking** or do voluntary work between school and university.

MY GLOSSARY

journey	n.	旅程, 旅行, 行程
	v.	旅行
match	n.	比赛; 火柴; 对手
recreational	adj.	娱乐的, 消遣的
cultural	adj.	文化的; 和养动植物有关的
sightseeing	n.	观光, 游览
adventure	n.	冒险; 奇遇
	v.	冒险; 尝试
explore	v.	探测, 探险; 考察, 探究
distant	adj.	遥远的, 疏远的
extreme	adj.	极端的, 极度的
ecotourism	n.	生态旅游

ethical	adj.	伦理的, 道德的
rainforest	n.	雨林
resort	n.	（度假）胜地
religious	adj.	宗教的; 虔诚的
Mecca	n.	麦加（沙特阿拉伯城市）
Muslim	n.	穆斯林
gap-year		间隔年（指青年在中学毕业后大学入学前或毕业之后工作之前做长期旅行的一段时期）
go backpacking		背包徒步旅行

2 **Read the text about travel and tourism. Match the type of tourism with its definition and an example.**

Type of tourism	Definition	Example
adventure tourism	holidays to resorts where there is snow	a foreign language
cultural tourism	to celebrate religious event or visit important religious places	voluntary work
ecotourism		Mecca for Muslims
educational tourism	to explore distant places or do extreme activities	monuments or museums
gap-year tourism	to learn about history, art and people's lifestyles	rainforests
health tourism		skiing or snowboarding
recreational tourism	to learn something	spa resorts
religious tourism	to look after your body and mind	the beach
sport tourism	to play or watch different sporting events	the Olympic Games
winter tourism	to take ethical and responsible trips to natural environments	trekking
	to relax and have fun	
	when young people go backpacking or do voluntary work between school and university	

3 **Read the text again and choose the correct answer to complete each sentence.**

1) People travel

   A for different reasons.   B to go on holiday.   C to get to work.

2) You can take

   A day and evening trips.

   B study and business trips.

   C theatre and cinema trips.

3) Tourism is travel

   A in your hometown.

   B to countries across the world.

   C to places where you don't live.

4) Ecotourism is ethical and responsible about

   A money.   B shopping.   C the environment.

5) The Olympics is a

   A sporting event.   B summer event.   C winter event.

6) A spa is a place you visit to

   A celebrate a religious event.   B learn something new.   C look after your health.

Listening

4 Listen to a conversation about where to go on holiday and match each member of the family with the type of tourism they would like from Exercise 2.

1) Dad *cultural*

2) Grandma _____

3) Hannah _____

4) Josh _____

5) Mum _____

6) Zoe _____

5 Complete the conversation below between a travel agent and a customer with expressions from the box. Then listen and check your answers.

Any ideas	How about	I agree	I quite fancy
I really want to	let's see	Personally, I'd like	Why don't you

Travel agent: (1) *Any ideas* about where you want to go on holiday this summer, Mrs Brown?

Customer: Well, (2) _____ have a proper family holiday this year.

Travel agent: OK, there are some good all inclusive package holidays by the sea.

Customer: Mmm! (3) _____ going somewhere different this year.

Travel agent: (4) _____ taking a city break?

Customer: (5) _____ it, but I think the kids might be bored.

Travel agent: (6) _____ combine a city break with something for the kids like Euro Disney?

Customer: That's a good idea, (7) _____, but isn't Euro Disney really expensive?

Travel agent: Well, (8) _____ if there are any special offers on at the moment.

Speaking

6 Look at the pictures about different holiday destinations in Exercise 1 and role play a conversation between a travel agent and a customer. Try to use expressions from Exercise 5.

Student A: You are a travel agent. Ask questions about what kind of holiday the customer wants this year.

Student B: You are a customer. Answer questions about what kind of holiday you want this year. When you finish, change roles.

Tourism is a multi-billion dollar business with hundreds of millions of travellers arriving in **destinations** across the world every year, but there's a lot more to tourism than just the tourists.

Before you even leave home you probably use a number of services. You book your trip through a **tour operator**, if it's a **package holiday**, or a travel agent, if you want to buy products and services like flights separately. These days, many people book directly online with companies that offer both **organised** and **independent** travel. You usually need to **purchase** airline, train, ferry and coach tickets to your holiday resort **in advance** to **reserve** a seat and get a good price. If you're **hiring** a car, it's also a good idea to book in advance, but you can arrange local transport like taxis and buses when you're there. You also need to book **accommodation** to be sure to stay where you want, when you want. There is a wide range of **options** for different people and pockets: from luxury hotels to roadside motels, family-run guesthouses or B&Bs (Bed and Breakfasts), to self-catering apartments to youth hostels. You can decide about hospitality (catering and entertainment) during your holiday, unless you book it with your accommodation. B&B means you get breakfast included in the price of your stay. Half board, usually only **available** at hotels, means breakfast and dinner are included. Full board means breakfast, lunch and dinner are included. This option is common on package or **cruise** ship holidays to keep the cost down, as are all **inclusive** leisure activities such as sport, shopping and live shows. Most places have a Tourist Information Point where they give you free information about what to see and do and how to get around. Organised trips often have travel reps (**representatives**) on hand to help you, but you can also pay a local tour guide to take you sightseeing or show you **tourist attractions**.

destination	n.	目的地, 终点	
tour operator		包价旅游承办商; 旅行社	
operator	n.	操作员; 技工; 管理者; 报务员	
package holiday		包价旅游	
organised	adj.	有组织的, 组织起来的	
independent	adj.	独立的, 自主的, 独自的	
purchase	v.	购买	
in advance		提前, 预先	

reserve	v.	保留, 预订
hire	v.	租用; 雇用
accommodation	n.	住处, 膳宿; 和解
option	n.	选择
available	adj.	可利用的, 可得到的
cruise	n.	乘船游览; 巡航, 巡游
inclusive	adj.	包含……在内的
representative	n.	代表; 众议员; 典型
tourist attraction		旅游景点

7 **Complete the table with the correct information after your reading.**

Hospitality

Accommodation (Where to stay)	Catering (Where to eat)	Entertainment and leisure (What to do)	Jobs (Who does what)	Transport (How to travel)	Holiday types (What kind of holiday)
luxury hotels	bed and breakfast	sport	tour operator	plane	package holiday

8 **Read the text again and answer the questions.**

1) How many travellers arrive in destinations across the world every year?

2) How can you book holidays?

3) Why do you need to purchase tickets for airlines, trains, ferries and coaches in advance?

4) If you're hiring a car, is it a good idea to book in advance?

5) When can you arrange local transport, if you're hiring a car as your transportation?

6) Is there a wide range of different accommodation options? What are they?

7) Which kind of accommodation includes breakfast, lunch and dinner?

8) Is full board a common option? Why?

9) Do you pay for information from Tourist Information Points?

10) Who can take you sightseeing or show you tourist attractions?

Writing

9 Complete the online travel search information according to holidays you like.

Holidays you like

Trip Search...

HOLIDAY TYPE (only tick [✓] one)

Package holiday ☐   Transport & accommodation ☐

Transport only ☐   Accommodation only ☐

Transport, accommodation and car hire ☐

TRANSPORT (tick one or more)

Flight ☐

Car hire ☐   Ferry tickets ☐

Train tickets ☐   Coach tickets ☐

Leaving from:_____ Departure date:_____ Time:_____

Going to:_____ Return date:_____ Time:_____

ACCOMMODATION (only tick one)

Hotel ☐   B&B ☐

Motel ☐   Apartment ☐

Guesthouse ☐   Youth hostel ☐

CATERING (only tick one)

Full board ☐   Breakfast only ☐

Half board ☐   Self-catering ☐

ENTERTAINMENT & LEISURE INTERESTS (tick one or more)

Adventure ☐	Extreme sport ☐	Trekking ☐	Languages ☐
Culture ☐	Museums ☐	Art galleries ☐	Music & drama ☐
Ecotourism ☐	Natural world ☐	Conservation ☐	Shows ☐
Educational ☐	Arts & crafts ☐	Cooking ☐	
Gap-year ☐	Backpacking ☐	Voluntary work ☐	
Health ☐	Spa resorts ☐	Yoga & meditation ☐	
Religious ☐	Events ☐	Places ☐	
Recreational ☐	Seaside ☐	Shopping ☐	
Sport ☐	Playing ☐	Sightseeing ☐	

10 There is a problem with an online booking system. Write an email to the website operators giving them the information in your trip search. Use the expressions in the box for your help.

I want to book...	I'd like to return on... at...
I'd like to travel by...	I'd like to book accommodation in a... with (catering)
I'm leaving from...	I'm interested in... tourism
I'm going to...	In particular, I'd like to...
I want to leave on... at...	

Learning Objectives

Upon completion of the unit, students should be able to:

• categorise tourism organisations and describe e-marketing strategies of a travel agency;

• apply the vocabulary on tourism organisations, advertising, promotion and marketing;

• give advice on holidays for different groups of people;

• write an advert to market holidays to targeted customers including 4 Ps.

Unit 2 Tourism Organisations, Promotion and Marketing 13

Starting Off

1 **Look at these company logos and answer the questions.**

1) Do you recognise these company or organisation logos?

2) What type of companies or organisations are they?

3) Do you know Thomas Cook? If not, please check on line.

Reading 1

Tourism **organisations** fall into three **categories**. Firstly they can be non-governmental organisations or a **charity** like the World Tourism Organisation, a United Nations' organisation which **promotes** "the development of responsible, **sustainable** and universally **accessible** tourism" (UNWTO). Secondly, they can be government organisations like Britain's national tourism agency, Visit Britain, which markets British tourism at home and abroad. Thirdly, they can be **private** sector organisations like Thomas Cook, which promote and sell holidays for **profit**.

We can separate this last group into three more categories. Independent companies have one or more **branches**, which can often be close to each other. They sell their holidays to people locally and market them by word of mouth. Miniple companies have several branches in different areas, which sometimes use different trade names and they have a head office, which can manage the organisation's marketing strategy centrally. **Multiple** agencies have branches in all major towns and cities and they can be part of very large tourism sector companies. They market holidays on the basis of competitive prices or special offer packages. In addition to this, travel agents can be members of trade **associations**, organisations representing travel companies who can help with marketing and protect customers' rights. Of course nowadays many people prefer online do-it-yourself tourism to any of these organisations.

organisation	n.	组织, 团体（等于 organization）	private	adj.	私人的, 私立的, 私营的
charity	n.	慈善（团体）; 施舍	profit	n.	利润; 利益
promote	v.	促进; 提升; 推销; 发扬	branch	n.	分支; 分公司; 分部
sustainable	adj.	可持续的	multiple	adj.	许多的; 多重的; 多样的
accessible	adj.	易接近的; 可进入的; 可理解的	association	n.	协会, 联盟, 社团

category | n. | 种类, 分类; [数] 范畴

2 Read the text about tourism organisations and complete the table.

Category of tourism organisation	Example	Type of organisation and what they do
non-governmental organisations / a charity	UNWTO	
		markets British tourism at home and abroad
private sector organisations		
independent		have one or more branches, …
miniple		
multiple		
trade associations		

3 Write the equivalent word or phrase in your language.

1) charity: _____ 6) to market: _____

2) sustainable: _____ 7) word of mouth: _____

3) to promote: _____ 8) trade name: _____

4) profit: _____ 9) head office: _____

5) branch: _____ 10) competitive: _____

4 **Read the short descriptions of National Trust sites and match a person with a place to visit.**

❦ National Trust

a **Wellbrook Beetling Mill:** Do you like trying new crafts? Do you enjoy going for walks in the country and having picnics on the <u>lawn</u>? Then come to this water-powered linen <u>mill</u> in Northern Ireland. It's open 2–6 p.m. March to September.

b **South Foreland Lighthouse:** Can you imagine living and working in a lighthouse on the White Cliffs of Dover overlooking the sea, at the time of the first international radio transmission? Find out what it's like and learn about Marconi and Faraday's early experiments, March to October, 11 a.m. to 5.30 p.m.

c **Red house, Kent:** If you love looking at beautiful things, this is the place for you. You can see William Morris's art nouveau furniture, Edward Burne-Jones's original <u>artwork</u>, or try relaxing and playing games in the <u>landscaped</u> garden. Open March to December 11 a.m. to 5 p.m.

d **Theatre Royal, Suffolk:** Do you have a passion for drama? Visit Britain's last Regency theatre. You can see the amazing hand-painted ceiling. It's just like the sky! Then watch a 19th-century-style play. Open February to November, Tuesday and Thursday p.m., Saturday and Sunday a.m. Entrance is free. You only pay for performances.

e **Dunster Castle, Somerset:** Are you mad about history? Explore the secret passage in the medieval castle. Discover the Lovers' Bridge in the gardens. Go bat-watching in the great hall. Find out about the lives of Dunster's noble families. Visit the gardens all year round, 11–4 in winter, 11–5 in summer. The castle opens March to October 11–5.

1) ☐ⓐ Claudia is quite artistic and she loves trying new things. She doesn't like science, but she likes being in the country.

2) ☐ David likes art and architecture and he also enjoys relaxing and playing games. He hates learning about history.

3) ☐ Gwen is mad about history and drama. She hates being outside and doesn't really like gardens or nature.

4) ☐ Holli is very romantic and likes investigating mysteries and nature-watching. She's also quite interested in history and gardening.

5) ☐ Mick has a passion for science and loves finding out about how things work. He doesn't like going to museums or to theatres.

Listening

5 Complete this text about the National Trust with the words and expressions in Reading 1. Be careful to use the appropriate grammatical form. Then listen and check your answers.

The National Trust is a (1) _charity_ and a non-(2) _____ organisation, which (3) _____ British tourism to artistic, historical and natural sites in a (4) _____ way. It has two (5) _____, one in London and another in Swindon, as well as hundreds of (6) _____ all over the UK. Places with the (7) _____, "National Trust" (8) _____ themselves through the image of conservation and heritage. However, many of the thousands of visitors to National Trust sites hear about them by (9) _____ from friends, colleagues or relatives. They provide great days out for the whole family as you can enter many sites for free and you can also hire venues for special events at extremely (10) _____ prices.

Dunster Castle, Somerset

6 Listen to the interview with a travel agent about his company's e-marketing strategies and decide if these sentences are true (*T*) or false (*F*). Correct the false ones.

	T	F
1) They use TV and radio adverts. *No, they don't use them because they are too expensive.*	☐	☑
2) They sometimes place ads in newspapers or magazines they think their target customers buy.	☐	☐
3) They advertise in specialist travel brochures, leaflets or tourism guides.	☐	☐
4) Their main marketing area is online.	☐	☐
5) They use a combination of low-cost e-marketing strategies.	☐	☐
6) They don't like social networking sites.	☐	☐
7) They never advertise on search engines.	☐	☐
8) Banners are not competitive and they don't always reach the target customers.	☐	☐
9) It's not possible to book online.	☐	☐
10) They have great word of mouth marketing through their forum.	☐	☐

Speaking

7 **Work in pairs. Follow the instructions below, and then swap roles.**

Student A: Ask your partner about his/her interests. Then choose the best activity for him/her from Exercise 4.

Student B: Tell your partner about your interests and what you like and don't like doing. Do you agree with Student A's choice of activity for you?

8 **Look at the list of different kinds of media advertising in the box and discuss which you think you could use to market holidays for each group of people.**

newspapers	TV	the Internet	magazines	travel brochures
leaflets	tourism guides	social networking sites	websites	online forum
radio	search engine banners		word of mouth	

1) A big family who want an all inclusive package holiday

2) A retired couple interested in history and heritage

3) A group of friends who want an adventure holiday

4) A young married couple

5) A gap-year student

6) A young person looking for a cheap city break

7) A group of friends looking for a last minute offer

8) You!

Student A: *I think we could use newspapers or tourism brochures to market an all inclusive package holiday to a big family.*

Student B: *I don't agree. I think everybody uses the Internet these days, so maybe we could use a search engine banner or a website.*

Reading 2

People are often unclear about exactly what marketing is, and **confuse** it with **advertising** and promotion, both important parts of marketing. Advertising brings a product or service to the attention of **customers** through the media, e.g. newspapers, TV, or the Internet, to **persuade** them to buy it. Promotion keeps a product or service in the minds of customers and helps **stimulate** their demand for it, often through advertising. Marketing is altogether more **complex**. It is all the activities **involved** in making sure that customers buy a product or service by understanding and meeting their needs. Traditionally this is called the four Ps marketing mix: Product; Price; Place; Promotion. In other words you need to market the right product at the right price in the right place and in the right way if you want to sell it. You could add one other P to this: you need to sell it to the right people.

You can **identify** the right people through a process called market **segmentation**. This is when you group together people with similar needs and wants to identify your target customers so you can successfully market your product to them. There are many ways of doing this, for instance: by the amount of money people have (do they want budget or luxury holidays?); by the kind of activities they're interested in (**heritage**, nature or adventure); by their circumstances (are they single, a couple, or a family?); by their age (18–25 or 60+); and by the kind of tourists they are (independent or **pampered**).

MY GLOSSARY

confuse	v.	使混乱, 使困惑	involve	v.	包含; 牵涉
advertise	v.	做广告, 登广告; 宣传	identify	v.	确定; 鉴定
customer	n.	顾客	segmentation	n.	分割; 割断
persuade	v.	说服, 劝说	heritage	n.	遗产; 传统
stimulate	v.	刺激; 鼓舞, 激励	pampered	adj.	骄奢的
complex	adj.	复杂的; 合成的			

9 **Match the terms with the correct definitions.**

1) advertising   a ☐ It keeps a product or service in the minds of customers and helps stimulate their demand for it.

2) promotion   b ☐ It makes sure that customers buy a product or service by understanding and meeting their needs.

3) marketing   c ☐ It brings a product or service to the attention of customers through the media to persuade them to buy it.

10 Read the text and answer the questions.

1) Give three examples of advertising media.

2) Give an example of promotion.

3) Name the four Ps of the marketing mix.

4) Name the fifth P.

5) Name the process of grouping together people with similar needs and wants in marketing.

6) Give some examples of this.

Writing

11 **Look at the picture of a holiday destination. You are a member of the marketing team for a big travel company. Choose your target customers and write an advert marketing the holiday to them. Remember the 4 Ps (Product, Place, Price and Promotion) and decide what media to advertise through. In your advert, include details of:**

- suitable activities for customers to do;
- facilities and services you offer;
- the price (with offers/discounts);
- the length and period of the holiday (try to suit it to your customers);
- other information to attract your customers.

Learning Objectives

Upon completion of the unit, students should be able to:

- identify types of transport in tourism;
- apply the vocabulary on transport in tourism;
- communicate with people working in the tourism industry about types of transport;
- write an email recommending types of transport for a potential customer.

Starting Off

1 **Discuss the following questions in groups.**

1) Can you mention any types of transport in your mind?

2) How did you travel in China or abroad? By public transport, taxi or car?

3) Which type of transport would you prefer if you travel in China? Why?

Reading 1

2 **Read the four paragraphs about different types of transport and match them with the pictures.**

1) ☐ Air travel is a fast way of travelling both for **domestic** and international journeys. Some **airline** companies **operate scheduled** flights, when take-off and landing are at major airports in major cities. Because departure and arrival times are regular and **guaranteed**, tickets can be expensive. **Alternatively**, there are cheap **charter** flights when a travel company buys all the seats on a plane and sells at a discounted price. Charter airlines and low-cost scheduled airlines often operate from more accessible local airports and fly direct to holiday resorts, particularly in peak season. You usually need to buy tickets in advance. It is also possible to buy round-the-world tickets where you stop off at different global destinations. There is a limit to how much luggage passengers can carry and it takes time to check-in for flights due to security checks. Nowadays many people try to avoid taking too many flights because they aren't good for the environment.

2) ☐ Sea travel can be a clean alternative to air travel. **Ferries** operate from one mainland destination to another, or between islands, departing and arriving at major ports. You can often take your car on ferries and there are no limits on the luggage you can carry. Journeys are long compared to flights and they can be quite expensive, especially if you sleep in a **cabin** overnight. You can buy tickets directly from the ferry companies or through tour operators, usually in advance. You can also take a luxury cruise, but they are generally quite expensive, all-inclusive packages.

3) ☐ Rail travel also has a low environmental **impact** and is a very **flexible** and **convenient** mode of transport because you can buy tickets in advance or just turn up at the station. Price varies a lot according to distance and destination. Luggage allowance is limited on trains, but on long distance trips you can book a bed to sleep in, called a **berth**. There are also young person's rail passes for travelling around Europe and many countries have cheap or **subsidised** rail travel.

4) ☐ Road travel can be by car or by **coach**, but neither is very environmentally friendly. Car travel is very convenient because you can choose your own departure and arrival points and times, and take as much luggage as your vehicle can carry. The cost is **generally** low apart from fuel and any **tolls**, but travel time can be long. Alternatively you can arrive at your destination and hire a car on arrival, but this can be expensive. Coaches, like trains, follow timetables and you need to buy tickets in advance to be sure of a seat. Journeys can be slow and arrival times are **unpredictable** because of traffic. They are however cheap and convenient, with stops at both major and minor destinations.

MY GLOSSARY

domestic	adj.	国内的; 家庭的	impact	n.	影响; 效果
airline	n.	航空公司	flexible	adj.	灵活的; 柔韧的
operate	v.	经营; 操作	convenient	adj.	方便的, 近便的
scheduled	adj.	预定的; 已排程的	berth	n.	卧铺
guarantee	v.	保证, 确保	subsidised	adj.	资助的, 补贴的
alternatively	adv.	要不, 或者	coach	n.	长途巴士; 教练
charter	n.	（飞机、船等的）租用	generally	adv.	通常; 一般地, 普遍地
ferry	n.	渡船; 摆渡	toll	n.	通行费
cabin	n.	船舱; 客舱; 小屋	unpredictable	adj.	不可预知的

3 **Match these words and expressions from the text with their definitions.**

1) charter flight   a ☐ a plane leaving at the same time each day or each week

2) environmentally friendly   b ☐ a plane journey organised by a company that buys all the seats

3) fuel   c ☐ a special train ticket you can buy to travel around a specific area for a specific period of time

4) landing   d ☐ bags and suitcases that you take on a journey

5) luggage   e ☐ not causing damage to the natural world

6) peak season   f ☐ the activities to protect a country, building or person against attack or danger

7) rail pass   g ☐ the time of year when a lot of people go on holiday

8) scheduled flight   h ☐ what we put in a car to make it go, e.g. petrol or diesel

9) security checks   i ☐ when an airplane leaves the ground and starts flying

10) take-off   j ☐ when the plane returns to the ground at the end of a journey

4 **Read the four texts again and answer the questions. Be noted that some have more than one answer.**

Which type of transport:

1) can be quite expensive if you travel overnight?

2) has a low environmental impact?

3) has a luxury version with all-inclusive packages?

4) has limits on passenger luggage?

5) has long security checks?

6) has unpredictable arrival times?

7) is convenient because you can choose your own route?

8) is not environmentally friendly?

9) operates between mainlands or islands?

10) has guaranteed departure and arrival times?

Listening

5 **Listen to the conversation and finish the exercise.**

1) The conversation takes place _____.

A in a ticket office   B in a travel agency   C in a tour operator's office   D on the phone

2) What kind of ticket does the customer want to buy?

A A single ticket.   B A flight ticket.   C A rail ticket.   D A cruise ticket.

6 **Listen to the conversation again and complete it with the missing information.**

Woman: Hello, I'd like to buy a ticket to (1) _____ please.

Ticket officer: Is that a (2) _____ or a (3) _____ ticket?

Woman: A (4) _____ please.

Ticket officer: When do you want to (5) _____?

Woman: Now.

Ticket officer: And when do you want to (6) _____?

Woman: Today, please. (7) _____ is that?

Ticket officer: A (8) _____ day return ticket is (9) _____.

Woman:	What time is the next (10) _____?
Ticket officer:	It's at (11) _____ from platform (12) _____.
Woman:	Thank you.

7 **Read these airport procedures and put them in the order you should do. The first and the last are done for you. Then listen to the recording and check your answers.**

a ☐*1*   Arrive at the airport and go to the correct check-in desk.

b ☐   Check in your luggage and take your boarding pass.

c ☐   Give the airline staff your passport and booking information.

d ☐   Present your boarding card and identification for inspection at passport control.

e ☐   Proceed to the departure gate when it opens.

f ☐   Put your hand luggage and coat through the security check.

g ☐*8*   Show your passport and boarding card to staff before boarding.

h ☐   Walk through the metal detector.

WINGS AIRLINE

FIRST CLASS

WINGS AIRLINE

Gate **19**

Gate Closes **20:42**

Seat **27**B

Gate **19**

Gate Closes **20:42**

Seat **27**B

Class First Class

Departure New York JFK

Arrival London LHR

REF No 00800597 524

FIRS

Speaking

8 **Role play conversations at the ticket office. Use the conversation from Exercises 5 and 6 for your help. Then swap roles.**

9 **Read the conversation below between an airline steward and a customer and complete it with the expressions from the box. Then role play the conversation with a partner.**

A window seat, please.	~~Here they are.~~	Just one.
Yes, I did.	Good, it doesn't weigh very much.	

Airline steward: Good morning, can I have your passport and booking information, please?

Customer: (1) _____ *Here they are* _____ .

Airline steward: Would you like a window or an aisle seat?

Customer: (2) _____

Airline steward: Did you pack your bag yourself?

Customer: (3) _____

Airline steward: Put your bag on the scales, please.

Customer: (4) _____

Airline steward: How many pieces of hand luggage have you got?

Customer: (5) _____

Airline steward: Here are your passport and boarding pass. You need to go to Gate 3 at 14.20.

Reading 2

You're at your holiday destination, and now you need to continue your journey. Taxis are quick and **efficient** for short journeys, but they can be expensive. Many charge per **passenger**, piece of luggage, as well as **surcharges** for airport and night time journeys. If you want to be free to travel when and where you like, car hire can offer good value. You pay a daily or weekly rate for hiring a car, plus fuel costs and you choose the kind of car you want, but most are bad for the environment. **Adventurous** tourists can rent a motorbike, **moped** or bicycle. These are cheaper and also more environmentally-friendly, but watch out for traffic or people stealing your bike! For people on a budget, public transport is a good and green option. Cities usually have a choice of underground, buses, trains and sometimes **trams** and cable cars too. In small towns, the options are more limited. Cost and convenience vary a lot in different places, so look out for special offers like **combination** tickets, weekend or all-day travel passes. Of course if you want to save your money and the planet, you could always walk!

MY GLOSSARY

efficient	*adj.*	有效率的; 有能力的
passenger	*n.*	旅客, 乘客
surcharge	*n.*	额外费用
adventurous	*adj.*	爱冒险的; 大胆的

moped	*n.*	助动车, 机动脚踏两用车
tram	*n.*	轨道电车
combination	*n.*	组合, 结合

10 **Match these transport symbols you may see in airports with the words in the box.**

buses	car hire	parking	taxis	trains	underground

1) _____

2) _____

3) _____

4) _____

5) _____

6) _____

11 Complete the table below according to the text.

Mode of transport	Positive things about it	Negative things about it
taxi		
		bad for the environment
motorbike	adventurous	
public transport	good for people on a budget	cost and convenience vary a lot

Writing

12 Suppose you work at a tourist information office. Your boss shows you an email from Mr Humphries. Please read it first and then identify who it is to.

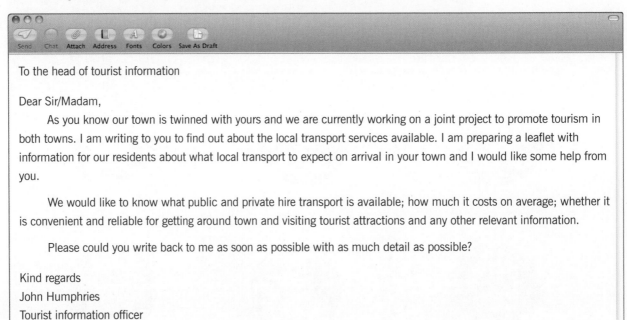

To the head of tourist information

Dear Sir/Madam,

As you know our town is twinned with yours and we are currently working on a joint project to promote tourism in both towns. I am writing to you to find out about the local transport services available. I am preparing a leaflet with information for our residents about what local transport to expect on arrival in your town and I would like some help from you.

We would like to know what public and private hire transport is available; how much it costs on average; whether it is convenient and reliable for getting around town and visiting tourist attractions and any other relevant information.

Please could you write back to me as soon as possible with as much detail as possible?

Kind regards
John Humphries
Tourist information officer

13 Your boss asks you to complete the survey about transport available in your town.

PUBLIC TRANSPORT	
[Please tick your answers]	
• What public transport is available?	☐ underground ☐ buses ☐ trams ☐ trains ☐ cable cars ☐ other _____
• Are they reliable services?	☐ yes, usually ☐ not always ☐ sometimes ☐ not usually
• How much does an average journey cost?	_____
• Are there a lot of stops around town?	☐ Yes, there are. ☐ No, there aren't.
• Are they convenient for tourist attractions?	☐ Yes, they are. ☐ Yes, some are. ☐ No, they aren't.
• Where can you buy tickets for public transport?	☐ on board ☐ at the stop/station ☐ other _____
• Are there any problems with these modes of transport?	☐ traffic ☐ overcrowding ☐ crime ☐ other _____

14 Your boss asks you to write a reply to John Humphries's email, using the information in your transport survey. Be honest about the local transport available, but be as positive as possible. Remember you want tourists to visit your town!

Dear Mr Humphries,

Thank you for your recent email. In answer to your questions...

_____

_____

_____

_____

Kind regards

Learning Objectives

Upon completion of the unit, students should be able to:

- understand factors to take into consideration when choosing accommodation in tourism;
- apply the vocabulary on accommodation in the tourism industry;
- communicate with a hotel receptionist about services of accommodation;
- describe services and facilities related to a hotel stay.

Starting Off

1 Discuss the following questions in groups.

1) Where do you usually stay when you go on holiday?

2) Can you make a list of all the different types of tourist accommodation you can think of?

3) Which type of accommodation would you prefer if you travel in China? Why?

Reading 1

1) barge

2)

3)

4)

Nowadays, the choice of tourist accommodation to suit your taste, **budget** and destination is endless. At the high end of the market there are hotels, offering rooms and meals. Motels are similar, except they are for motorists. So they are generally on major roads and always provide parking, but not always meals. B&Bs, or **guesthouses**, differ from hotels as they are usually small, less expensive, owner-**occupied**, family-run businesses without staff on call 24/7. Alternatively, holiday villages are popular with families who may be travelling on a budget. They offer a choice of self-catering accommodation from small wooden cabins or **chalets** to studio apartments to large holiday **villas**, all in modern resorts with many **leisure** and recreational services available on site.

Private holiday **rental** offers a wide **variety** of accommodation. Then there are timeshares, where several people own accommodation they can use at **specific** periods each year. To avoid getting bored with the same destination, how about doing a house **swap**, where people spend holiday in each others' houses?

Hostels provide a low-cost, self-catering alternative to hotels, and appeal to young travellers, as the shared dormitories make it easy to meet people. Increasingly, universities offer campus accommodation in students' halls of residence during the holidays. This is the type of accommodation you often find on study holidays, but it can also be a cheap and sociable way to take a city break.

If you're looking for an adventure on a budget, campsites are perfect. You can take your own tent, or even stay in a traditional round Mongolian **yurt** or a tall Native American **tepee**. For more comfort, there are also **caravans** and **campervans**, which enable you to enjoy a holiday on the move. Finally, if you like to combine transport and accommodation, why not try a **barge**, a long flat boat which travels on rivers and canals, or a **yacht** if you prefer the sea.

5)

6)

7)

8)

MY GLOSSARY

budget	*n.*	预算
guesthouse	*n.*	宾馆, 小型家庭旅馆
occupy	*v.*	占用, 占领; 从事; 使忙碌; 专心
chalet	*n.*	（瑞士的）小木屋
villa	*n.*	别墅
leisure	*n.*	闲暇, 休闲
rental	*n.*	租赁
	adj.	租借的
variety	*n.*	多样; 种类

specific	*adj.*	特定的, 明确的; 具有特效的
swap	*n.*	交换; 适合交换的东西
yurt	*n.*	（游牧地区的）圆顶帐篷
tepee	*n.*	（北美印第安人的）圆锥形帐篷
caravan	*n.*	大篷车; 宿营车;（穿越沙漠的）旅行队, 商队
campervan	*n.*	露营车
barge	*n.*	驳船
yacht	*n.*	游艇, 快艇

2 **Write the names of the types of accommodation in the boxes in the picures.**

3 **Read the text again and choose the correct answer.**

1) Hotels are accommodation at the
   A budget end of the market.   B high end of the market.   C low end of the market.

2) Guesthouses and B&Bs are different from hotels because they are generally run by
   A families.   B one person.   C staff 24/7.

3) You can visit a timeshare
   A all year round.   B at a specific time each year.   C only in summer.

4) House swapping helps you to
   A avoid boredom.   B avoid cooking.   C make friends.

5) Hostels appeal to

    A couples.   B families.   C young people.

6) Campus accommodation is available for tourists to rent during

    A the holidays and term time.   B the holidays.   C term time.

7) For comfortable and mobile campsite holidays, try

    A campervans.   B tents.   C tepees.

8) Which of these isn't a kind of boat?

    A Barge.   B Yacht.   C Yurt.

Listening

4 **Listen to a man checking in at a hotel and complete the hotel registration form.**

HOTEL INTERCONTINENTAL
PARIS

1) Surname: _____
First Name: _____

2) Address: _____
City: _____ Country: _____ Postal Code: _____

3) Telephone: _____ Mobile: _____
Email: _____

4) Type of Room:
☐ single room   ☐ double room single occupancy   ☐ double room with bath
☐ shower   ☐ bath & shower

5) Type of Board: ☐ full board   ☐ half board   ☐ B&B

6) Arrival Date: _____ Departure Date: _____ Total: _____ nights

I authorise the Paris InterContinental Hotel to charge my credit card with the full amount due.

7) Credit Card Type: _____ Signature: _____ Room Number: _____

5 Listen to the telephone conversation between a hotel guest and the receptionist. Put a tick (✓) under "G" for all the services the guest requests, and under "R" for all the services the hotel receptionist says are available at the hotel. Then complete the table with the information from the listening.

Service	G	R	Specific information about the service
à la carte restaurant			*Open 12–2 lunchtime and 7–10 for dinner. You need to book a table for dinner.*
complimentary toiletries			
en suite bathroom			
hairdryer			
hotel reception staffed 24/7			
internet access			
ironing service			
laundry service			
room service			
safe in the room			

Speaking

6 Role play the conversation between the hotel receptionist and the customer and complete the hotel registration form in Exercise 4 with your partner's information.

7 Role play a conversation between a guest and a receptionist asking and answering about different services. Take notes about the available services, and then swap roles. Use the expressions in the box for your help.

Another thing...	I'm calling from/about...
Can I help you with anything else?	Is it possible for me to have...?
I can't find the...	It/They should be...
I'd like to book... for 8 p.m.	There are a few things missing...
I'm afraid we don't have...	You need to book...

Reading 2

The kind of **facilities** and services available to you on holiday varies greatly according to your choice of accommodation. **Catered** accommodation such as hotels, guest houses and B&Bs is generally **categorised** using a star system which varies from country to country.

Generally one star tends to **indicate** budget accommodation, offering basic facilities such as **en suite** bathrooms and TVs in all the rooms and services such as breakfast, drinks and daily room cleaning by **chambermaids**.

Two stars may **additionally** offer guests bath towels, **complimentary toiletries** such as shower gel, a reading light, and a credit card payment facility.

Three star hotels often also provide a hairdryer and telephone in every room as well as internet access either in a public area or in the room, laundry and ironing services, and the hotel reception is staffed for around 14 hours by **bilingual** staff, speaking English and the **native** language.

The reception of a four star hotel should be manned for up to 18 hours, have a refrigerated minibar or room service for drinks, and an **à la carte** restaurant. There would also probably be a lift and more comfortable furniture.

Finally five star luxury accommodation should offer a reception area staffed 24/7 by multilingual staff, a doorman to welcome guests, **valet** parking, a porter to take luggage to your room, and a safe in the room for valuables. There are often gym and spa facilities available too.

MY GLOSSARY

facility	*n.*	设施, 设备
cater	*v.*	提供餐饮及服务
categorise	*v.*	将……分类
indicate	*v.*	表明, 指出
en suite		[法]成套的; 接连的
chambermaid	*n.*	女服务员
additionally	*adv.*	额外地, 此外; 又, 加之

complimentary	*adj.*	赠送的; 称赞的
toiletry	*n.*	浴室用品; 化妆品
bilingual	*adj.*	双语的
native	*adj.*	本国的; 土著的
à la carte		[法]按菜单点菜
valet	*n.*	帮助客人停车

8 Complete the table about accommodation services and facilities.

★	★ ★	★ ★ ★	★ ★ ★ ★	★ ★ ★ ★ ★
en suite bathroom	*complimentary toiletries*	*hairdryer*	*reception manned for up to 18 hours*	*reception area manned 24/7*

9 Read the text again and label the pictures with the hotel facilities you see.

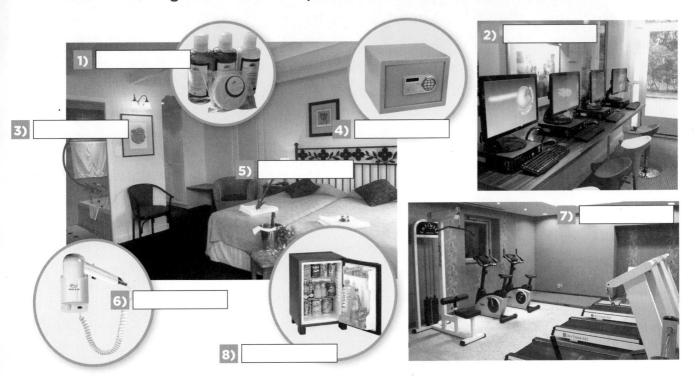

1)

2)

3)

4)

5)

6)

7)

8)

10 Match the hotel staff with the service they provide.

1) chambermaid

2) doorman

3) multilingual staff

4) porter

5) waiter

a ☐ welcoming guests

b ☐ restaurant

c ☐ luggage service

d ☐ reception

e ☐ cleaning rooms

Writing

11 Now write a postcard to a family member or friend telling them about your hotel stay. Use your notes about the services and facilities in Exercises 7 and 8.

Dear _____,

I'm staying at the Grand Palace Hotel and the services and facilities are excellent. For example there is...

UNIT 5 Planning and Booking a Holiday

Learning Objectives

Upon completion of the unit, students should be able to:

• grasp different ways and aspects of planning and booking a holiday;

• apply vocabulary on booking a holiday;

• communicate with travel agents about booking and planning a holiday;

• write a review of a hotel or any other holiday-related services.

Starting Off

1 **Discuss the following questions in groups.**

1) Are there any national holidays in China? What are these holidays?

2) Did you have experiences of booking a holiday for yourself, friends or family?

3) What do you usually take with you when you travel around?

Reading 1

Nowadays there are plenty of different ways to book a holiday. Because of advances in technology you can now book holidays over the Internet; by **teletext**, a system providing news and other information through the TV; over the phone or by going into a travel agency. However you choose to book, you should ensure you have everything you need before departing for your holiday. This might include: **valid** travel documents such as passports, **identity** cards or visas for entry into specific countries and maybe your driving **licence** if you intend to drive your own or hire a car; travel tickets for planes, ships, trains or coaches and most airlines now expect you to check-in online before you fly and bring your printed **boarding card** with you to the airport. You should also consider purchasing some form of travel insurance to cover your costs in case your plane is delayed, cancelled, you lose

any personal items or there is an emergency whilst you are on holiday. You can buy this independently or directly from your travel agent or travel provider. If you are travelling abroad, some banks like you to inform them, otherwise they may block your **credit** and **debit** cards when you try to use them overseas. However, it is always wise to take some currency or a pre-paid debit card with you in case there are any problems.

Travel to certain countries requires **immunisation** against diseases. These vary from country to country, as each has different risks to people health-wise, but you should check with your doctor around six weeks before going on your holiday to discuss possible **vaccinations** you may need for your destination.

teletext	n.	图文电视	credit	n.	信用
valid	adj.	有效的; 合法的	debit	n.	借记, 借方; 借项
identity	n.	身份			
licence	n.	许可证, 执照	immunisation	n.	免疫
boarding card		登机牌	vaccination	n.	接种疫苗; 种痘

2 **Read the text about planning and booking a holiday and choose the correct answer.**

1) Which of the following are ways of booking a holiday?

    A By phone.　　　　B In a travel agency.　　C Over the Internet.　　D All of these ways.

2) Which of the following do you only need for entry into specific countries?

    A Identity card.　　　B Passport.　　　　　C Visa.　　　　　　　D None of these.

3) You are expected to check in and print a boarding card before going to

    A an airport.　　　　B a bus station.　　　　C a ship's port.　　　　D a train station.

4) You might need travel insurance in case you

    A decide not to travel.　　　　　　　　B have an emergency on holiday.
    C lose something before travelling.　　　D miss your plane.

5) If you don't tell your banks you are going abroad, what might they do?

    A Block your cards.　　　　　　　　　B Close your account.
    C Not give you any currency.　　　　　D Refuse you credit.

6) Some countries require immunisation against diseases

    A when you return from your holiday.　　B six weeks before travel.
    C during the holiday.　　　　　　　　　D before and after the holiday.

3 **What do you need the following for? Talk to a partner.**

boarding card	driving licence	passport	immunisation	visa

I need a boarding card to get onto a plane.

Listening

4 **Listen and complete the travel agent's booking form with the information you hear.**

> AURORA TRAVEL AGENCY BOOKING FORM
>
> Type of holiday:
> ☐ package   ☐ flight only   ☐ accommodation   ☐ other (please specify: _____)
> Destination: _____
> Specific dates: _____
> Type of accommodation: _____
> Transfers: _____

5 **Listen again and complete the second part of the conversation with the missing information in the box.**

> So, I'll need a 50% deposit now and the balance at least 14 days before the holiday date.
> So your holiday is a two-week, all-inclusive package to the Marmais Resort.
> Return flights; transfers to and from Dalaman Airport; a self-catering apartment, which will be cleaned once a week and use of a communal swimming pool.
> Now your passport numbers and expiry dates.   No problem. You can email them to me.
> I also need both your dates of birth.   Can I have the full names of all the people travelling, please?

Travel agent:	(1) _____
Customer:	My name is Andrew Jones and my girlfriend's name is Karen Miller.
Travel agent:	(2) _____
Customer:	My date of birth is 5 March 1985 and Karen's is 8 June 1989.
Travel agent:	(3) _____
Customer:	Oh! I'm afraid I haven't got them with me.
Travel agent:	(4) _____
Customer:	Ok. Thanks.
Travel agent:	(5) _____
Customer:	What's included in that?
Travel agent:	(6) _____
Customer:	Perfect!
Travel agent:	(7) _____
Customer:	OK. Here's my credit card.

6 Listen and complete the hotel feedback form based on the conversation between a hotel receptionist and the customer checking out.

ACORN HOTEL FEEDBACK FORM

Customer name: _____

Room number: _____

Please indicate how much you enjoyed your stay overall:

☐ not at all ☐ It was OK. ☐ quite a lot ☐ very much

Please tell us what you liked about your stay:

_____

Please tell us what you would change or improve about your stay:

_____

Which of the following reflect your check-out experience?

The bill was correct. / incorrect. _____

Staff were helpful. / unhelpful. _____

It was quick and easy. / slow and complicated. _____

Other (please specify). _____

Would you consider a return visit to our hotel?   ☐ yes   ☐ no   ☐ maybe

Would you recommend our hotel to friends or family?   ☐ yes   ☐ no   ☐ maybe

Thank you very much for your valuable suggestions and comments.

Speaking

7 Take turns to role play a travel agent and a customer booking a holiday. Refer back to Exercises 4 and 5 for your help.

Customer: *I'd like to book a...*

Travel agent: *OK...*

FAQ

Q: What time is check-in and check-out?
A: Check-in time is 3 p.m. and check-out is 11 a.m.
Q: Can we use the facilities either side of these times?
A: Yes, you can use the facilities before checking in and after checking out of your room.
Q: Are early check-in and late check-out available?
A: Yes, for an **additional** fee. Please ask at reception.
Q: What time is breakfast served?
A: Breakfast is between 7 a.m.–9.30 a.m. midweek and 8 a.m.–10 a.m. on a weekend.
Q: What time is dinner served?
A: Dinner is served from 7 p.m.–9.30 p.m. every day. We strongly **recommend** you pre-book.
Q: How do I make changes to my room **reservation**?
A: If you booked through the hotel, contact us, otherwise contact your travel agent directly.
Q: Can I **upgrade** my room?
A: If a **suitable** room is available, you can upgrade your room for an additional fee.
Q: What is your **cancellation policy**?
A: We require a minimum of 48-hour notice **prior to** scheduled arrival date for a full **refund**.
Q: Is parking available at the hotel?
A: Yes, the hotel offers free valet and self-parking.

If you have any other questions, please contact reception.

MY GLOSSARY

additional	*adj.*	附加的, 额外的
recommend	*v.*	推荐, 建议
reservation	*n.*	预约, 预订; 保留
upgrade	*v.*	给 (飞机乘客或宾馆客人) 升级
suitable	*adj.*	适当的; 相配的

cancellation	*n.*	取消; 删除
policy	*n.*	政策, 方针
prior to		在……之前, 先于
refund	*n.*	退款, 退税

8 **Read the text and decide if these sentences are true (T) or false (F).**

	T	F
1) You can't use hotel facilities before checking in or after checking out.	☐	☐
2) You have to pay if you want to change your check-in or check-out time.	☐	☐
3) Breakfast is at the same time every day of the week.	☐	☐
4) It's a good idea to book a table at the restaurant.	☐	☐
5) The hotel can change all room bookings.	☐	☐
6) It isn't possible to upgrade your room.	☐	☐
7) If you cancel more than 48 hours before your stay, you will get all your money back.	☐	☐
8) Parking doesn't cost anything.	☐	☐

9 **Match the words that mean the same.**

1) additional	a ☐ appropriate
2) fee	b ☐ annulment
3) recommend	c ☐ booking
4) reservation	d ☐ charge
5) upgrade	e ☐ extra
6) suitable	f ☐ improve
7) available	g ☐ obtainable
8) cancellation	h ☐ reimbursement
9) refund	i ☐ suggest

Writing

10 **Imagine you are Mr Lewis. Write an online review for the Acorn Hotel based on the information in the feedback form in Exercise 6. You should:**

- give your review a title, which reflects your overall experience;
- describe the good points;
- describe the things to improve/change;
- say if you would return/recommend the hotel to others;
- provide any further useful information.

Learning Objectives

Upon completion of the unit, students should be able to:

• grasp major forms of written and oral communication in tourism industry;

• apply the vocabulary on written and oral communication;

• communicate with standard phrases on phone calls in tourism;

• write emails and business letters with proper format.

Starting Off

1 **Discuss the following questions in groups.**

1) Which one do you think is more important, written communication or oral communication?

2) How can you improve your communication skills?

3) Do you think communication is important in your daily life? (List examples to explain.)

Reading 1

Communication is **vital** within the tourism sector to inform, present, promote and sell. It is **essential** that communication tools are used **effectively** to provide customers with clear information and details about these experiences on offer.

Written Communication

Written communication is an important part of working in the tourism sector, whether it is replying to an enquiry, confirming a booking, filling in a **registration** form or composing a promotional **brochure**. Apart from evaluating which form of written communication is the most suitable for your purpose, it is also essential to decide whether you need to use a formal or informal tone. Emails and **memos** are usually informal, while business letters are normally more formal. A form is usually **neutral** in style. There are various standard formats and practices to follow.

Emails

Email (**electronic** mail) is a system of sending and receiving text messages digitally over a computer network and between personal computers or similar devices. It is fast, convenient and eco-friendly, as long as you do not print out masses of emails unnecessarily. Emails are so direct and instant that they have changed the way businesses communicate and have led to a decrease in the formality of business **correspondence**.

Memos

A memo (or memorandum – plural: memorandums/memoranda) is a short note informally **conveying** minimal information from one person, department or office to another. They can be on paper or electronic. Memos are used to tell employees about changes in procedures, rules or policy, or else for a specific purpose like a request to attend a meeting.

- The subject should be brief and specific, relating to the purpose of the memo.
- Memos do not usually contain greetings or closing **salutations**.
- The text should be clear and to the point. Use short sentences.
- Use **contractions** and **abbreviations**. **Imperatives** can often be used.
- State the most important points first and then move on to the details.

Forms

Many commercial documents are often forms, such as booking and registration forms, customer data forms, and payment forms. A form, whether it is printed or online, is made up of fields which need to be filled in with specific information. It is important to follow the **instructions** carefully. For example, many printed forms require you to write in block capitals or to use only black ink. Online forms, on the other hand, often have required fields – normally marked with an **asterisk** – which must be filled in otherwise the form is not valid and cannot be submitted.

MY GLOSSARY

vital	*adj.*	至关重要的
essential	*adj.*	基本的, 必要的
effectively	*adv.*	有效地, 生效地
registration	*n.*	注册, 登记
brochure	*n.*	小册子, 手册
memo	*n.*	备忘录
neutral	*adj.*	中立的, 中性的
electronic	*adj.*	电子的

correspondence	*n.*	通信
convey	*v.*	传达, 表达
salutation	*n.*	称呼, 称呼语
contraction	*n.*	缩写形式
abbreviation	*n.*	缩略词
imperative	*n.*	命令; 祈使语气
instruction	*n.*	指令, 说明
asterisk	*n.*	星号标记符

2 Read the text and the following email and answer the questions.

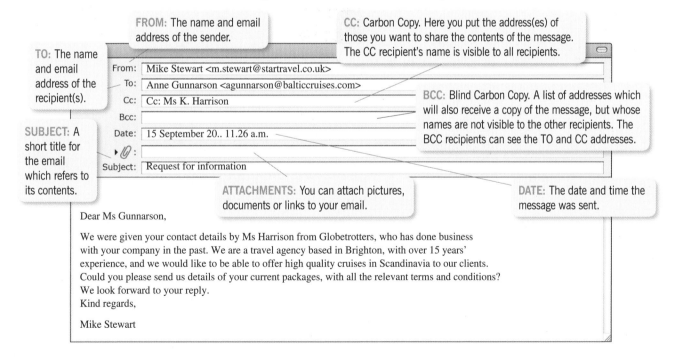

1) What are informal forms in written communication?

2) If you attach pictures, documents or links to your email, what is it called?

3) What's the difference between BCC and CC?

3 **Read the email in Exercise 2 and find the equivalent expressions.**

1) Ms Harrison gave us your name.

_____

2) Our travel agency has been in business for more than 15 years.

_____

3) We are interested in offering...

_____

4) Would you mind sending us...?

_____

5) Looking forward to hearing from you.

_____

6) Best regards

_____

4 **Read the text and the following memo and answer these questions.**

Cardiff Tourist Office Memo

From: Jackie Pladstow, General Manager
_To:_ All staff
Date: 18 February 20.
Subject: Staff Meeting

There'll be a staff meeting at 12.30 p.m.
on Thursday 21st February.
This is preparation for welcoming the
fans for the next Six Nations Rugby
Match at the Millennium Stadium. Over
25,000 fans will arrive for the match so
we need to be ready.
Thanks for your co-operation.

1) Is a memo an internal or external document?

2) Why should you use short sentences?

3) What formalities do memos generally not contain?

4) Who is writing the memo? And to whom?

5) What is the memo about?

6) Why is the staff meeting important?

5 Match these expressions to those with the same meaning in the form below and complete it with your contact details.

1) given name _____

2) family name _____

3) ZIP code _____

4) sex _____

5) mark _____

Please fill in this form with your contact details.

* **First name**	(1)		**City**	(5)	
* **Last name**	(2)		* **Postcode**	(6)	
Title	(3)		**Date of birth**	07 11 1980	(DD MM YYYY)
* **Email**	(4)	@btinternet.co.uk	**Gender**	✓ M F	
* **Address**		21 Long Drive			

Please tick this box if you do not wish to receive our weekly newsletter. ☐
* *required fields*

Listening

6 Listen to a phone conversation and answer these questions.

1) What is the purpose of the phone call?

2) Who will pay for the hotel room?

3) How much does the room cost?

4) How will James confirm the booking?

7 Listen to the phone conversation again and write down the missing words/expressions.

James: Sundance Hotel. How can I (1) _____ ?

Janet: Good morning. This is Janet from Spencer & Clark. (2) _____ speak to Mr Lang, please?

James: Hello Janet. James (3) _____ .
How are you?

Janet: Fine. Thanks. I'm (4) _____ book a single en suite room, from the 20th to the 22nd of July, 2 nights in total, in the name of Mr Moore.

James: Just a second, let me check… Yes, that's fine. We have a room (5) _____ .

Janet: Good. Mr Moore will be our guest so will you charge the room at our preferential rate of £75 per night. (6) _____ breakfast?

James: Of course. I'll send you confirmation of your (7) _____ by email in a few minutes.

Janet: OK. Thanks very much.

James: You're (8) _____ . Bye.

Janet: Bye.

8 Read and listen to the phone conversation again. Write down the expressions for these functions. Then complete the table with other expressions you can think of.

Answering the phone	Introducing yourself	Asking to speak to someone	Saying why you are calling

9 Listen to this automated information system and match the number to press to the correct option. There are two extra options you do not need.

E ☐ luggage allowances on board

A ☐ special deals

B ☐ change a booking

1	2 ABC	3 DEF
4 GHI	5 JKL	6 MNO
7 PQRS	8 TUV	9 WXYZ
*	0 +	#

F ☐ make a booking

C ☐ talk to an operator

G ☐ lost luggage claims

D ☐ special assistance

10 Read the instructions and practise the telephone conversation.

You work for the travel agency GetAway.
Call the local tourist office.

You work for the local tourist office.
Answer the phone.

Ask to speak to Mr Greyson.

Say Mr Greyson is not in the office.
Ask if the caller wants to leave a message.

Leave a message asking him
to call you back in the afternoon.

Tell the caller you will give
Mr Greyson the message.

Thank the person.

Close the conversation.

Close the conversation.

11 Now practise mini-telephone conversations with a partner for these situations. Remember to swap roles.

Caller	Receiver
You want to speak to the hotel manager at Hotel Horizon, but he/she is out. Ask when you should call back.	You work for Hotel Horizon. The manager is on holiday and will return next Friday.
You call Mr Clarkson at Ewans Coach Hire to ask about the costs of hiring a coach. You need the information urgently.	You work at Ewans Coach Hire. You can send the caller a price list immediately by fax or email.
You call Star Tours to ask for a copy of their new catalogue. You need it urgently.	You work for Star Tours. The new catalogue will be available next week. You will send it then.

Reading 2

Oral communication, whether face to face, on the phone or **via** the web, is a vital part of business today. Therefore good oral communication skills — in both your mother tongue and in English — are essential to help you make a good **impression**, express your ideas clearly and get ahead in the world of work.

Telephone calls

Making and receiving telephone calls in a foreign language is one of the hardest things to do in the workplace. As we are unable to see the person we are speaking to, we cannot use the usual non-verbal **clues**. Eye contact, facial expressions and body language are all unvoiced ways of communicating and help us understand our **interlocutor**.

Fortunately, phone calls follow certain standard phrases. Learning to pronounce them well will help you go a long way in mastering telephone skills and reduce the **anxiety** that is so common at first **attempts**.

Geoff Riley from the travel agency TravelEase calls a tour operator to have more details about a last-minute holiday offer for Santorini, Greece.

Receptionist

Good afternoon. Greek Adventures. How may I help you?

Good afternoon. This is Geoff Riley from TravelEase. I'd like to speak to Maggie Smith, please.

I'm sorry, but she's out of the office. Can I take a message?

Yes, thank you. I'd like to have a few more details regarding your last-minute offer for Santorini.

OK. I'll put you through to Ms Wilkins. She can help you.

Thank you.

Ms Wilkins

Hello, Mr Riley. Joanne Wilkins speaking. You wanted some information about our offer to Santorini.

Yes, that's right. I'd like to receive some more details about the hotel and whether it's also possible to leave from Manchester Airport.

OK. Both Manchester and Leeds are possible. I'll email you the full details straightaway.

Thanks. My email is g.riley@travelease.co.uk.

Great. I'll send it now. Thank you for calling. Goodbye.

Goodbye.

Geoff

via	*prep.* 经由, 通过	interlocutor	*n.*	对话者, 谈话者
impression	*n.* 印象	anxiety	*n.*	焦虑, 担心, 紧张
clue	*n.* 线索, 提示	attempt	*n.*	尝试, 试图

12 Read the text and answer the questions.

1) How would good oral communication help a person at workplace?

2) What is the hardest thing to do in workplace according to the text?

3) Are there standard phrases that phone calls could follow?

13 Read the phone call above and find the equivalent expressions.

1) My name is Geoff Riley. *This is Geoff Riley.*

2) Can I speak to...? _____

3) She isn't here. _____

4) Would you like to leave a message? _____

5) This is Joanne Wilkins. _____

6) Could I have...? _____

Writing

14 Read the description and the example of a business letter, and then discuss with your partner how to write a business letter.

Business Letters

A business letter is a formal means of communication. When you write a business letter, make sure it is clear, correct, courteous, convincing and complete. Before writing a business letter you always need to know exactly what type of letter you are writing, why you are writing and what you want to achieve. This will help organise what you intend to say. Ideally your letter should not be too long, in order to respect the limited amount of time the recipient might have available.

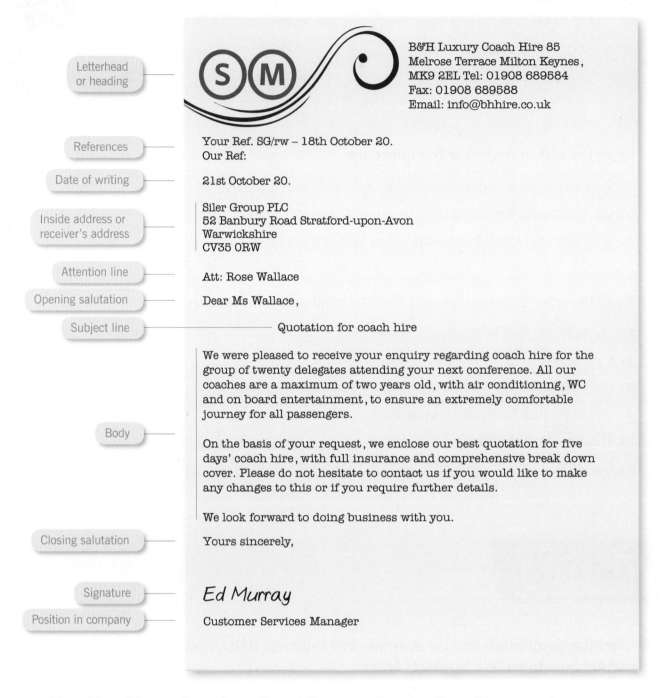

Letterhead or heading

B&H Luxury Coach Hire 85
Melrose Terrace Milton Keynes,
MK9 2EL Tel: 01908 689584
Fax: 01908 689588
Email: info@bhhire.co.uk

References

Your Ref. SG/rw – 18th October 20.
Our Ref:

Date of writing

21st October 20.

Inside address or receiver's address

Siler Group PLC
52 Banbury Road Stratford-upon-Avon
Warwickshire
CV35 0RW

Attention line

Att: Rose Wallace

Opening salutation

Dear Ms Wallace,

Subject line

Quotation for coach hire

Body

We were pleased to receive your enquiry regarding coach hire for the group of twenty delegates attending your next conference. All our coaches are a maximum of two years old, with air conditioning, WC and on board entertainment, to ensure an extremely comfortable journey for all passengers.

On the basis of your request, we enclose our best quotation for five days' coach hire, with full insurance and comprehensive break down cover. Please do not hesitate to contact us if you would like to make any changes to this or if you require further details.

We look forward to doing business with you.

Closing salutation

Yours sincerely,

Signature

Ed Murray

Position in company

Customer Services Manager

Discussion: After reading, please discuss these questions together with your partner.

1) What are the five Cs of a business letter?

2) Why do you think they are important?

3) Who is sending the letter?

4) What kind of company does he work for?

5) Who is the recipient of the letter and which company does she work for?

6) What is the purpose of the letter?

15 Imagine you were a hotel manager and you would like to write an email to confirm a reservation of 100 rooms with ABC Company who will hold a conference of over 200 people in your hotel. You should confirm the type of rooms, the conference room, buffet and other facilities with Mr Thomas, the manager of the company. Use the example in Exercise 14 and the following sample as your reference.

The Body of the Letter

Opening paragraph
The first paragraph states the purpose of the letter. It also refers to any previous correspondence or dealings.

Middle paragraph
The middle paragraph or paragraphs are the main points of the letter, for example giving information about a company, specific details of a request or an explanation for a problem. Each point or theme should be in a new paragraph.

Closing paragraph
This suggests a course of action and tells the reader what response is required.

Dear Sirs,

We are a leading luxury hotel group in Italy, with over 30 hotels across the country, and we would like to propose our hotels for your customers interested in visiting il bel paese.

All of our hotels are located in breathtaking countryside, such as those in Tuscany and Le Marche, or they are situated in the historical centres of our country's most famous cities, such as Turin, Rome and Palermo. We have been in operation for over 10 years and have built up an excellent reputation for high quality amenities and top class customer service. Our restaurant in Rome, for example, has just been awarded a Michelin star. Please browse our website www.grandihotels.it at your convenience in order to view the luxury experience we offer.

Hoping to start welcoming your customers in the near future, we look forward to hearing from you.

Yours faithfully,

Learning Objectives

Upon completion of the unit, students should be able to:

- understand the history, nature, cultural activities and life style of different international tourism destinations;
- apply the vocabulary on international tourism destinations;
- make plans for holiday destinations and activities;
- write a "Must Do" guide about a tour place.

Starting Off

1 **Discuss the following questions in groups.**

1) Is there any international tourism destination in your mind if you have time and money to plan a trip?

2) Which international destination is on the top of your travelling list? Why?

3) Do you recognise these tourist destinations in Europe? Match the names with the pictures.

> Monte Carlo   Lapland   Ibiza   Greenland   Algarve

1)

2)

3)

4)

5)

Reading 1

Europe is **extremely** varied. Greenland, in the north, is largely in the **Arctic** Circle with deep **fjords**, **glaciers** and **icebergs**, and summer sees endless days and winter endless nights. Many people take nature and cultural holidays to see wildlife like polar bears, **reindeer**, and whales and experience the unique **Inuit** culture.

Northeast is Lapland, Finland's northern wilderness providing amazing views of the Northern

Lights, **Aurora Borealis**, a **spectacular** colourful display of lights caused by solar wind entering the earth's atmosphere. Summer is great for hiking and white water rafting adventures, **whilst** winter tourism includes **snowmobiling**, **sled** safaris, skiing and visits to Santa Claus's Village at Christmas.

Europe also offers sun, sea and sand in its southern **Mediterranean** countries. Spain's four **Balearic** Islands have everything for recreational tourism. **Ibiza**, for example, is the choice for young, trendy, party-going tourists, while **Mallorca** is a favourite for family beach holidays, but also great for mountain hikes. **Menorca** is a quieter island, with UNESCO **archeological** and natural sites. Finally, **Formentera**, the smallest island, is the destination for tourists who just want to relax.

The **Algarve** region, on the west coast of **Portugal**, is well-liked too by beach tourists because of wide sandy beaches, natural bays and **breathtaking** cliffs.

For the wealthier, more **chic** tourist, the French Riviera remains fashionable. In Nice, tourists can combine recreation and culture: sunbathing, visiting Impressionist art galleries, eating delicious French cuisine, practising water sports and drinking cocktails.

Along the coast is the small, but nevertheless rich nation of **Monaco**. It's famous for **casinos**, its **glamorous** royal family and the formula one racing track at **Monte Carlo**, but don't go there unless you're looking for luxury tourism!

MY GLOSSARY

extremely	*adv.*	非常, 极其; 极端地
Arctic	*adj.*	北极的
fjord	*n.*	[地理] 峡湾(等于 fiord)
glacier	*n.*	冰河, 冰川
iceberg	*n.*	[地理] 冰山; 显露部分
reindeer	*n.*	驯鹿
Inuit	*n.*	因纽特人; 因纽特语
Aurora Borealis		[地物] 北极光
spectacular	*adj.*	壮观的, 引人入胜的
whilst	*conj.*	当……的时候, 与……同时
snowmobiling	*n.*	雪上汽车; 机动雪橇
sled	*n.*	雪橇
Mediterranean	*n.*	地中海 *adj.* 地中海的
Balearic	*n.*	巴利阿里群岛
Ibiza	*n.*	伊比沙岛(地中海西部)

Mallorca	*n.*	马略卡岛(西班牙)
Menorca	*n.*	梅诺卡岛(西班牙)
archeological	*adj.*	考古学的(等于 archaeological)
Formentera	*n.*	福门特拉岛(地中海西部)
Algarve	*n.*	阿尔加维(葡萄牙城市)
Portugal	*n.*	葡萄牙(欧洲西南部国家)
breathtaking	*adj.*	惊人的, 惊艳的
chic	*adj.*	优雅时髦的 *n.* 时髦; 独特风格
Monaco	*n.*	摩纳哥(欧洲西南部国家)
casino	*n.*	赌场; 游乐场; 俱乐部
glamorous	*adj.*	迷人的, 富有魅力的
Monte Carlo		蒙特卡洛(摩纳哥城市)、

2 **Read the text and complete the table.**

Country/Region	Type of tourism	Things to see and do
Greenland	nature or cultural	fjords, glaciers, icebergs; endless days in summer and endless nights in winter; wildlife like polar bears, reindeer and whales; experience the unique Inuit culture

3 **Match the words with their definitions.**

1) Aurora Borealis   a ☐ a journey to watch, take pictures of or hunt wild animals

2) fjord   b ☐ a very large mass of ice moving slowly

3) iceberg   c ☐ a thin strip of sea between high rocks typical of Scandinavian countries

4) glacier   d ☐ a luminous atmospheric display visible in the Northern Hemisphere

5) safari   e ☐ a large piece of ice moving in the sea with a small amount above the water

Listening

4 **Listen to a conversation between a travel agent and a customer about travel advice to the USA and complete the missing information.**

Travel agent: I just want to go through all the things you need to do before you leave for the USA.

Tourist: Sure, no problem.

Travel agent: First you have to check your (1) _____ is valid for at least (2) _____ months after you plan to return home.

Tourist: Yes, it is. Do I have to apply for a (3) _____ too?

Travel agent:	No, you don't. There's a visa waiver programme for all UK or EC passports, but you have to apply through ESTA, Electronic System for Travel Authorisation to the USA, online at least (4) _____ hours before your departure.
Tourist:	How long can I stay in the USA with this programme?
Travel agent:	You can stay for up to (5) _____ days.
Tourist:	OK. What about security at the airport?
Travel agent:	Security is very tight for all US travel, so you should arrive at the airport at least (6) _____ hours before your departure time.
Tourist:	Do I need (7) _____?
Travel agent:	Well, you don't have to be immunised against any diseases, but it's a good idea to get comprehensive travel insurance.
Tourist:	Right. How about money?
Travel agent:	The (8) _____ is dollars, but you don't need to take out money in advance because you can use credit cards and cash point machines, which Americans call ATMs.
Tourist:	OK. Thanks for all your help and advice.

5 Listen to the conversation again and complete the table below about what you need to and don't need to do when you travel to the USA.

Need to	Don't need to
check your passport is valid for at least six months after you plan to return home	apply for a visa

6 Listen to a passage about historical sightseeing tour and write the place names under each picture.

1) _____

2) _____

3) _____

4) _____

7 Listen again and complete the missing numbers.

Humans first lived in the British Isles about (1) _____ years ago, but Britain's most famous prehistoric monument and UNESCO world heritage site, Stonehenge, was probably built in Wiltshire at different times between (2) _____ and (3) _____ BC. The mysterious giant stones set in a unique concentric architectural design are a mixture of nearby sandstone and smaller bluestones from the Preseli Mountains in South Wales, about (4) _____ miles away. We don't know exactly how or why Stonehenge was built, but experts agree it was a ceremonial site for worship and burial and people continue to visit it every year to celebrate the summer solstice.

The Welsh, Irish and Scots originate from the Celts, Indo-European tribes who settled in Britain in about (5) _____ BC and the word probably comes from the Greek *keltoi*, meaning barbarian. The Romans successfully invaded and conquered Britain in (6) _____ BC, establishing the city of *Londinium*, now London, and in the southwest of England, *Aquae Sulis*, Bath Spa, one of the world's finest remaining examples of Roman thermal spas, with natural hot springs of (7) _____ °C.

To keep out the Scots, still regarded as barbarians, the Emperor Hadrian gave order to build Hadrian's Wall from stone and earth, which stretches (8) _____ km from coast to coast across northern Britain.

The Roman rule in Britain ended when the Anglo Saxons from northern Europe began to invade the island in the (9) _____ century AD.

The Vikings from Norway, Sweden and Denmark also invaded Britain in about the (10) _____ century AD, settling in central, northern and eastern England. The modern city of York in the north of England is site of the Jorvik Viking Centre, a settlement where Viking-age houses, workshops and artefacts were excavated.

The Normans conquered Britain with victory at the Battle of Hastings in (11) _____ bringing linguistic, architectural and political changes to Britain. They built mediaeval Motte and Bailey castles, which had raised earth, the "motte", under the castle which you could only access across a wooden drawbridge. Around it was a ditch, separating the castle from the "bailey", that is to say a courtyard surrounded by a wooden fence where servants, tradesmen and craftsmen lived. Windsor Castle, just outside London, the official royal residence for over (12) _____ years, is an excellent example of this kind of castles.

8 **Listen again and complete the table.**

Monument	Site	Period	Architectural details	Reason for building it
		prehistoric		
Bath Spa				
	coast to coast across northern Britain			
				a settlement
	just outside London			

Speaking

9 **Take turns to role play a dialogue between a travel agent and a customer. Give advice on what he/she needs/doesn't need to do or bring when travelling to China. Include the following information:**

- airport security;
- medical insurance;
- visa requirements;
- money.

Reading 2

The capital of India is Delhi and its largest city is Mumbai. The technology capital **Bangalore** is the third largest city. No one

Capital: New Delhi	**National independence:** 1947
Largest city: Mumbai	**Longest river: Ganges**
Population: estimated almost 1.3 billion	**Currency:** Indian **Rupee**
Official languages: Hindi and English	**National Sport:** Cricket

knows which country has the most English speakers in the world, some people say India, and other people say the USA. It is the seventh largest country in the world. It has borders with China, Butan, Burma, Nepal, Pakistan, Bangladesh and its longest river is the Ganges. It has the world's second biggest population: at the moment is almost 1.3 billion. Some people think that by the 2030 its population will be bigger than China's. Northeast India is the wettest place in the world. India achieved **independence** from the British **Empire** in 1947. The Indian Rupee is the national **currency**. The country's national sport is cricket.

The Taj Mahal

The Mughal emperor Shah Jahan built the Taj Mahal for his third wife who died when giving birth to their 14th child.

It took 22 years to build and 20,000 people worked on it. At different times of the day the colour of Taj Mahal changes. Don't miss this amazing sight!

Goa

Think Goa, think beaches! Kilometres and kilometres of beautiful coastal beaches. Beaches with five star luxury hotels or quieter beaches with just a few **shacks**. If you like sunbathing, Goa is the place for you!

Elephant Safari

You can see Indian elephants on roads and at temples. In the past, kings used them for transport and during wars, and they still work in forest moving trees. But how about going on an elephant safari? Jump on an elephant and ride out to see other native animals like tigers, **leopards** and monkeys!

MY GLOSSARY

Mumbai	*n.* 孟买（印度最大城市）	**independence**	*n.*	自主；独立性，自立性
Ganges	*n.* 恒河			
Rupee	*n.* 卢比（货币）	**empire**	*n.*	帝国；帝王统治，君权
Hindi	*n.* 北印度语	**currency**	*n.*	货币；流通
Bangalore	*n.* 班加罗尔（印度南部城市）	**shack**	*n.*	棚屋，小室
		leopard	*n.*	豹

10 Read the text and decide if these sentences are true (*T*) or false (*F*).

	T	F
1) The largest city in India is Bangalore.	☐	☐
2) India possibly has the largest English-speaking population in the world.	☐	☐
3) India is the largest country in the world.	☐	☐
4) India has land borders with 6 countries.	☐	☐
5) India has the world's largest population.	☐	☐
6) The wettest place in the world is in India.	☐	☐
7) The Taj Mahal was built in honour of the second wife of the Emperor.	☐	☐
8) On Goa beaches you can easily enjoy sunbathing.	☐	☐
9) Elephant safari is now forbidden.	☐	☐
10) Elephants are usually employed in heavy forest works.	☐	☐

11 Complete the text below with the missing words.

> young Indians capital third many

Bangalore is the (1) _____ biggest city in India. It is the information technology (2) _____ of India and its nickname is the Silicon Valley of India. This is because there are so (3) _____ IT companies in the city. The original Silicon Valley is in California, USA, where the IT business was born in the 1980s.

Another nickname for this city is Garden City. Many (4) _____ successfully achieve an IT degree, being considered some of the most brilliant minds in the IT industry worldwide.

Writing

12 Research and write a short "Must Do" guide about one of the places mentioned in this unit. Use Readings 1 and 2 as models. Include at least one:

- cultural activity;
- nature activity;
- leisure/entertainment activity;
- other useful or interesting pieces of information about the place (time of year to visit, special events, local transport, etc.).

旅游英语

Learning Objectives

Upon completion of the unit, students should be able to:

• grasp the definition, principles and development of ecotourism;

• apply the vocabulary on ecotourism;

• discuss the benefits and downsides of different types of ecotourism;

• write an email about an ecotourism holiday.

Starting Off

1 Discuss the following questions in groups.

1) What is ecotourism? Can you give us an example of ecotourism holiday?

2) What is the principle of ecotourism?

3) What are the benefits of ecotourism?

Reading 1

2 Read the text about ecotourism and match each paragraph with a heading.

A definition of ecotourism	Benefits and downsides	Organisations involved
The principles of ecotourism	The future of ecotourism	The history of ecotourism

1) *A **definition** of ecotourism*

Any form of tourism – adventure, sports, recreational, cultural or educational – can be based on the principles of sustainable tourism, because it **contributes** to and doesn't harm the environment it's in. However, ecotourism is a separate branch of tourism altogether, widely defined as: "responsible travel to natural areas that **conserves** the environment and improves the **well-being** of local people."*

2) _____

What most ecotourism holidays have in common is their **ecological sustainability**, their support for local **communities**, conservation of the environment and of natural resources, their **sensitivity** towards cultural diversity, and their educational focus.

3) _____

Ecotourism was developed to meet the needs of the increasing number of nature tourists who were also concerned about the environment. There was an early example of ecotourism in Kenya, East Africa in the 1970s, where people began paying to visit safari parks and the money was used for wildlife conservation. Other successful examples are the nature **lodges** in the rainforests of Costa Rica and Belize, and recent **expeditions** to Antarctica.

4) _____

The greatest danger with ecotourism lies in its popularity. The high number of people means there is a constant need for accommodation, transportation and natural resources, all of which can damage the environment and natural **habitats**.

* The International Ecotourism Society, 1990.

On the other hand, ecotourism also enables us to sustain and support communities and their economies by creating jobs and investing in conservation, development and education projects.

5) _____

Today many international non-profit organisations are involved in researching and promoting ecotourism. Some of the best known include the World Tourism Organisation, the World Travel and Tourism **Council**, Tourism Concern and the World Wildlife Fund. Yet ecotourism has become so profitable that there are also many commercial organisations now focusing on this **niche market**.

6) _____

Ecotourism is currently the fastest growing market in the tourism industry, but is it too late? Have we already **destroyed** too much of the planet with our environmentally unfriendly mass tourism? In the future will we have to limit the numbers of visitors and increase the cost of travel in order to preserve certain destinations?

MY GLOSSARY

definition	n.	定义	lodge	n.	原木住宅; 门房, 侧屋; 乡间小屋
contribute	v.	贡献, 出力			
conserve	v.	保存	expedition	n.	远征; 探险队
well-being	n.	幸福, 康乐	habitat	n.	[生态] 栖息地
ecological	adj.	生态的, 生态学的	council	n.	委员会; 会议
sustainability	n.	可持续性	niche market		缝隙市场, 有机会的市场
community	n.	社区; [生态] 群落	destroy	v.	破坏, 毁坏
sensitivity	n.	敏感, 敏感度			

3 Read the text again and try to write a definition for each of these expressions.

1) habitat _____
2) ecotourism _____
3) niche market _____

4) environmentally unfriendly _____
5) wildlife conservation _____
6) non-profit organisations _____

4 Read the text again and decide if these sentences are true (*T*) or false (*F*).

	T	F
1) Any form of tourism can be sustainable but that doesn't make it ecotourism.	☐	☐
2) Ecotourism usually has an educational focus.	☐	☐
3) The earliest form of ecotourism was in Belize.	☐	☐
4) The popularity of ecotourism can be a problem.	☐	☐
5) Ecotourism doesn't create jobs.	☐	☐
6) It is possible to make a lot of money from ecotourism.	☐	☐
7) Ecotourism is not a fast growing market in the tourism industry.	☐	☐

Listening

5 Complete the conversation below between a travel agent and a customer with the expressions from the box. Then listen and check your answers.

conservation projects	eco-resorts	environmentally friendly	solar-powered
natural disasters	raise awareness	renewable energy sources	carbon-neutral

Customer: Hello. I'd like some information about (1) _eco-resorts_ in the Maldives, please.

Travel agent: Certainly. They are owned and run by native Maldivian staff, who receive fair salaries.

Customer: What about my carbon footprint?

Travel agent: Well, you might have heard that the Maldives is trying to become the first (2) _____ country in the world and the eco-resorts are contributing to that by using (3) _____ such as wind, water and sun.

Customer: How does that affect the accommodation?

Travel agent: The luxury chalets are (4) _____ and extremely (5) _____.

Customer: Are there other ways in which the resorts promote sustainability?

Travel agent: Yes, part of the money you spend on your holiday goes into (6) _____ like cleaning the local coral reefs.

Customer: What about cultural and educational projects?

Travel agent: There are plenty of opportunities to interact with the locals and learn about the wealth of cultural diversity, which makes up these islands. There are also educational projects to (7) _____ of environmental threats to these islands from (8) _____ like tsunamis and hurricanes.

6 Listen to this conversation between a tour group leader and a travel agent planning a European trip and complete it with the questions. Then listen and check the answers.

Group leader: Hello, I'm planning to take a tour group over to northern Europe from the UK next year and I'd like you to recommend some itineraries.

Travel agent: 1) _Sure. Which period of the year would you like to travel and for how long?_

Group leader: Sometime in spring so the weather is not too hot, maybe for about three weeks.

Travel agent: 2) _____

Group leader: Well, it's quite a mixed group in terms of age and interests, so I want to include something that will appeal to everyone.

Travel agent: I'd certainly recommend Greenland to you, because you can see some amazing wildlife and you also get to take boat trips along the fjords.

Group leader: 3) _____

Travel agent:	I would say that Iceland is more suitable because of the geysers and hot springs. There are lots of modern spa resorts you could stay at.
Group leader:	4) _____
Travel agent:	The best time to see them is in winter, but if you go to remote regions like Lapland without artificial lights, it is sometimes possible to see them.
Group leader:	5) _____
Travel agent:	At that time of the year there are great hiking and white water rafting trips which are really good for developing a team spirit.

Speaking

7 **Are you a good ecotourist? Take this test and find out!**

When you're abroad, do you...

a learn words and phrases in the local language and try to use them?
Yes ☐ No ☐

b only visit places that are listed in your guidebook?
Yes ☐ No ☐

c use as much water as you want to wash your hair, body and clothes?
Yes ☐ No ☐

d travel by public transport, hire a bike or walk?
Yes ☐ No ☐

e ask people before taking photographs of them?
Yes ☐ No ☐

f act and dress in the same way as you would at home?
Yes ☐ No ☐

g buy goods produced locally and eat typical local food?
Yes ☐ No ☐

h stay in big luxurious multinational hotels?
Yes ☐ No ☐

8 **Now match these answers to the quiz. Do you agree with them?**

1) [a] It's a good idea. It shows real respect for the people and culture and is a great icebreaker.

2) ☐ It's a good way of supporting local communities and businesses and learning more about a place.

3) ☐ Travelling by public transport is a great way to meet local people, and reduce carbon emissions.

4) ☐ You should respect people's right to privacy and always ask before taking a photo of a person.

5) ☐ Use water carefully. It's a precious natural resource in many countries and Westerners tend to use and waste far more than local people.

6) ☐ Keep in mind that many luxurious hotels don't support local economies; they often exploit local people and the environment.

7) ☐ Guidebooks are useful for learning about a place before you go, but local people always know the best places to visit. Ask them!

8) ☐ Remember that people in different places have different ways of thinking, behaving and dressing and you should respect that. Always ask if you're unsure about taking shoes off or covering your head.

9 **Discuss your answers to the quiz. Use the expressions in the box for your help.**

To be honest...	Yes, I have / No, I haven't.
To tell you the truth...	I've always/never done it.
Have you ever...	I've never thought about it before.

Student A: *When you're abroad, do you learn words and phrases in the local language and try to use them?*

Student B: *Yes, I have always learnt a few words when I've been to another country even if it's only "please" and "thank you".*

Reading 2

10 **Read the texts and match a picture with each paragraph.**

1) ☐ Have you always wanted to **photograph** tigers in the wild? Why not take a wildlife photography holiday in India? You'll learn from a professional wildlife photographer and stay in jungle eco-lodges supporting sustainable wildlife parks staffed by

A

locals. Group sizes will be limited to three people.

2) ☐ Have you ever thought about taking a walking holiday in Ireland, combining sea, hills and forests? You'll stay in **solar-powered**, eco-friendly guesthouses, **hiking** in small groups, eating locally produced food, learning about Irish culture and nature from your guides and **socialising** with the locals in traditional Irish pubs.

3) ☐ Have you ever imagined **trekking** the Inca trail to Machu Picchu, **kayaking** the fjords of Chilean Patagonia and nature-watching on the Galapagos Islands? Local accommodation, hospitality and guides provide opportunities to **interact** and learn about Latin American people and cultures.

4) ☐ Have you ever wished luxury didn't cost the earth? Well it doesn't have to if you're relaxing in a new eco-resort in the Maldives, destined to be the first **carbon-neutral** country in the world. Your money will help finance coral cleaning, waste management, water conservation and renewable energy sources.

5) ☐ Have you ever wanted to get up close to a great white shark? Why not join a team of **marine** biologists in South Africa monitoring the sharks from boats and cages in the sea? You'll spend most of your time working with a small dedicated group of locals, learning about sharks and educating the general public about them.

6) ☐ Have you ever been on a volunteering holiday? Here's your chance! Come to Cambodia and teach sport, music, art or drama to disadvantaged children. You will live with local host families, learn about the culture and take sightseeing trips to beaches, temples and monkey **refuges**.

photograph	v.	拍照	kayak	v.	泛舟, 划皮艇
	n.	照片, 相片		n.	独木舟, 皮划艇
solar-powered	adj.	太阳能的	interact	v.	互相影响, 互相作用
hiking	n.	徒步旅行, 远足	carbon-neutral	adj.	碳平衡的
socialise	v.	参加社交活动; 使社会化	marine	adj.	海洋的, 海运的
trek	v.	艰苦跋涉	refuge	n.	收容所, 避难所

11 Read the texts again and complete the table with information in each category.

Country	Accommodation	Activities	Wildlife and natural habitats	Ecotourism elements
India	eco-lodges	photography	tigers	sustainable wildlife parks; group sizes limited to three

Writing

12 **Suppose you are a travel agent and you have received an email from a customer enquiring about one of the ecotourism holidays in Reading 2. Write a reply including the details below. Use the expressions in the box to help you.**

- activities (nature, adventure, culture, etc.);

- accommodation (eco-lodges, locally run guest-houses, host families, etc.);

- the principles of ecotourism on which your holiday is based (group sizes, local staff, local produce, sustainable energy sources, educational focus, transport, etc.).

I am writing in reply to your letter asking for information about...	As for the...
I would like to let you know that...	I hope that you find this helpful...

UNIT 9 New Tourist Destinations

Learning Objectives

Upon completion of the unit, students should be able to:

• figure out new tourist destinations in the world;

• apply the vocabulary describing tourist destinations;

• introduce a new tourist destination;

• write a description of a new tourist destination.

Starting Off

1 **Do you recognise these tourist destinations? Match the names with the pictures.**

the Dolomites   Angola   Morocco   Dubai   Gothenburg

1)

2)

3)

4)

5)

2 Do you know anything about these tourist destinations? If not, please search on line.

3 If you have chances, where would you like to go among these tourist destinations?

Reading 1

Global **economic crises**, concern for the environment, the threat of **violence**, as well as social trends, are just some of the things dictating our choice of new tourism destinations.

Angola, in West Africa, also has bitter memories of a 27-year civil war. This may be why Angola's sandy beaches, wildlife parks and **Portuguese** architecture have remained unspoilt by tourism, and it's now a hot new destination.

Morocco is just a short **budget** flight away from Europe, but culturally it's a long **haul**. Fill your senses with the smells, colours and sounds of North Africa: enjoy a hot steam bath in one of Tangier's **hammams**; take a trip to the ancient city of Marrakesh; and go on a camel ride in the Sahara Desert.

Alternatively, why not take a skiing holiday in the totally man-made resort of Dubai in the United Arab Emirates? It has soft **artificial** snow, ice **sculptures**, a short ski run and a sledding hill. Great for beginners, but not quite so good for advanced skiers or the environment, as it takes a lot of energy to create a snow world in the heat of the Middle East!

Meanwhile, in Sweden, a more familiar winter destination, the western city of Gothenburg has become popular for beach tourism. It has a beautiful coastline, excellent seafood, and it's much cheaper than the rest of the country, as well as being home to the biggest **amusement park** in Scandinavia.

If you really care about the environment and want to save money, take a "staycation", staying at home and visiting local museums, swimming pools and other attractions, rather than travelling abroad.

MY GLOSSARY

economic	*adj.*	经济的, 经济上的
crise	*n.*	危机, 紧要关头
violence	*n.*	暴力; 侵犯
Portuguese	*adj.*	葡萄牙的; 葡萄牙人的
budget	*adj.*	廉价的
	n.	预算

haul	*n.*	旅程; 拖曳
hammam	*n.*	土耳其浴室, 澡堂
artificial	*adj.*	人造的
sculpture	*n.*	雕塑
amusement park		游乐园

4 **Read the text and match these words and expressions with their definitions.**

1) budget flight   a   ☑ a cheap journey by air

2) sledding hill   b   ☐ a holiday where you remain at home and visit places in your own country

3) social trend   c   ☐ not been changed to be less beautiful or enjoyable

4) artificial   d   ☐ a small mountain where you ride a snow sledge down

5) camel ride   e   ☐ a change or development in people's lives and habits

6) staycation   f   ☐ a place where you can have a steam bath in Islamic countries, usually with separate baths for men and women

7) unspoilt   g   ☐ an excursion on camel

8) hammam   h   ☐ man-made, not natural

5 **Read the text again and decide in which destination you can do these things.**

Where can you…

1) admire ice sculptures? *in Dubai*

2) have a steam bath?

3) eat excellent seafood?

4) enjoy unspoilt sandy beaches?

5) go to the beach in a winter destination?

6) see Portuguese architecture?

7) ski in a hot country?

8) visit the Sahara Desert?

Listening

6 Listen to the radio interview with a travel agent and complete the table with the destinations that are in and out. Listen again and complete the missing information about reasons for change.

Argentina	Bogotá	Guyana	New York	The Philippines	Rio de Janeiro
Tasmania	Thailand	The Amazon	Québec	The Andaman Islands	The Maldives

Destination in 👍	Destination out 👎	Reasons for change
Bogotá	*Rio de Janeiro*	It's not as crowded, but it's full of trendy (1) *Latin American* nightlife and entertainment.
		It has unique (2) _____ and offers spectacular (3) _____ islands for great diving opportunities.
		People are tired of the over popularity. There are (4) _____, crystal seas and amazing corals and (5) _____.
		It's got a lovely (6) _____, great markets and designer boutiques, as well as (7) _____ and nightlife.
		It has undiscovered tropical (8) _____; rapids and (9) _____ for rafting; a table top mountain for climbing and abseiling.
		For (10)_____, the food is fresh, healthy, tasty and it's definitely different!

7 **Read and listen to the conversation below between a travel agent and a customer and complete it with the missing words.**

Customer: I want to travel to Brazil during the FIFA World Cup.

Travel agent: OK. There are various World Cup (1) _____ available or you can go as an independent traveller.

Customer: I'd prefer to be independent because I'm travelling with my girlfriend and she wants to do some (2) _____ and have a bit of a beach holiday too.

Travel agent: Well, the first thing you need to decide is which games you'd like to (3) _____. We have a list of all the (4) _____ and the possible teams who will be playing there.

Customer: I see. What about travelling around the country?

Travel agent: It depends a bit on how many games you want to see and where they are located, but you can (5) _____, fly or travel by public transport.

Customer: I'm not sure. What would you advise?

Travel agent: Once again, it depends on what type of holiday you want. Car hire is quite cheap and you're independent, but traffic is (6) _____ especially in the big cities. Air travel is more expensive, but more relaxing and public transport is fun but it will be extremely (7) _____ during the World Cup.

Customer: I think we'd like to hire a car there. Can we book accommodation through you as well?

Travel agent: Certainly! I'll (8) _____ some costs and dates and get back to you as soon as possible.

Speaking

8 **Take turns to role play conversations between a travel agent and a customer who wants to find out more information about the sporting events below. Use the conversation above and the information in Reading 2 to help you.**

- Olympic Games in…;
- Monaco Grand Prix;
- Tour de France;
- Cricket World Cup.

Student A: *I'd like to travel to the Monaco Grand Prix.*

Student B: *Are you interested in a package holiday or do you want to be an independent traveller?*

9 **Can you name these well-known international sporting events? Read the text and check your answers.**

1) _____   2) _____   3) _____   4) _____

Sports tourism to international sporting events is a growing trend in the tourism industry.

Probably the most popular international sporting events are bicycle races such as the **annual** Tour de France, which attracts 12 to 15 million **spectators** along the **route**. Tourists are mostly domestic, but they still travel many kilometres to watch and support their cycling heroes.

For international travellers the most popular events are the FIFA football World Cup and the Olympics, followed by the European Football **Championship**. For instance, around 3.18 million fans attended the 2010 FIFA World Cup in South Africa, the first African nation to host the championship, and there are hopes for even more tourists at the 2014 World Cup which will be held in football-crazy Brazil.

Other popular sporting events such as the **Rugby** Union World Cup and the Cricket World Cup, which both happen every four years, and the **Formula** 1 Gran **Prix** also draw a large number of international visitors. The Monaco Grand Prix, alongside the US Indy 500 (Indianapolis 500) and the French Le Mans, is one of the most famous motor racing **fixtures** of the year, attracting 200,000 visitors in just four days!

So why do people like sports tourism? Surprisingly, the more sport we watch on TV, the more we want to watch live. Sports tourism is much more **appealing** in general these days, as events offer more comfort and entertainment as well as cheap travel options such as low-cost airlines. The kind of person participating in sports tourism rather depends on the sport they're watching, but statistics show the majority are young, middle-class people aged 18–35. However, rugby and cricket fans tend to be older and wealthier, athletics fans younger and on a tighter budget, while followers of Formula 1, usually older, richer and male.

annual	*adj.*	年度的, 每年的		formula	*n.*	公式, 方程式
spectator	*n.*	观众; 旁观者		prix	*n.*	[法] 奖金; 价格
route	*n.*	路线, 航线		fixture	*n.*	比赛, 赛事; 设备
championship	*n.*	锦标赛; 冠军称号		appealing	*adj.*	吸引人的, 有吸引力的
rugby	*n.*	英式橄榄球				

10 Read the text again and choose the correct answers to complete the sentences.

1) Sports tourism is becoming
A expensive.　　　　　B less popular.　　　　　C more popular.

2) Most of the visitors to the Tour de France are
A foreign.　　　　　B French.　　　　　C local.

3) In 2010 South Africa was the first African host of
A the FIFA World Cup.　　　B the Olympics.　　　C the Rugby World Cup.

4) Indianapolis, Monaco and Le Mans are all venues for
A cricket.　　　　　B motor racing.　　　　　C horse-racing.

5) Sports tourism is more appealing nowadays because events offer more
A comfort.　　　　　B discounts.　　　　　C celebrities.

6) Generally athletics fans
A are older.　　　　　B are women.　　　　　C don't have a lot of money.

11 Read the text again and complete the table.

Sport	Important Competitions	When it takes place	Type of tourists
cricket			
			domestic
		annually	
	World Cup		
		every four years	

Writing

12 You are a travel agent and you have received the email below from head office asking you to briefly describe five new travel destinations/activities for people in Italy. Work in small groups to plan and write a reply.

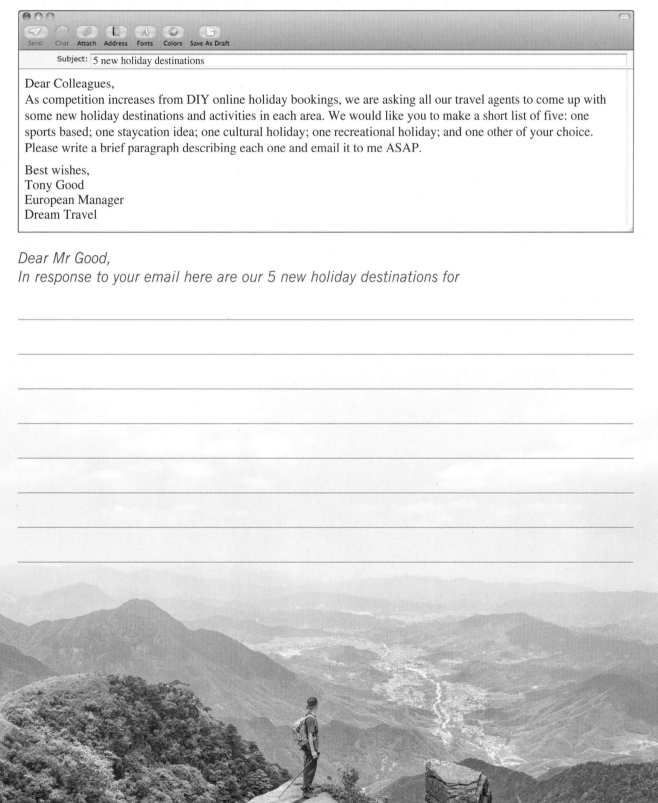

Send Chat Attach Address Fonts Colors Save As Draft

Subject: 5 new holiday destinations

Dear Colleagues,

As competition increases from DIY online holiday bookings, we are asking all our travel agents to come up with some new holiday destinations and activities in each area. We would like you to make a short list of five: one sports based; one staycation idea; one cultural holiday; one recreational holiday; and one other of your choice. Please write a brief paragraph describing each one and email it to me ASAP.

Best wishes,
Tony Good
European Manager
Dream Travel

Dear Mr Good,
In response to your email here are our 5 new holiday destinations for

----

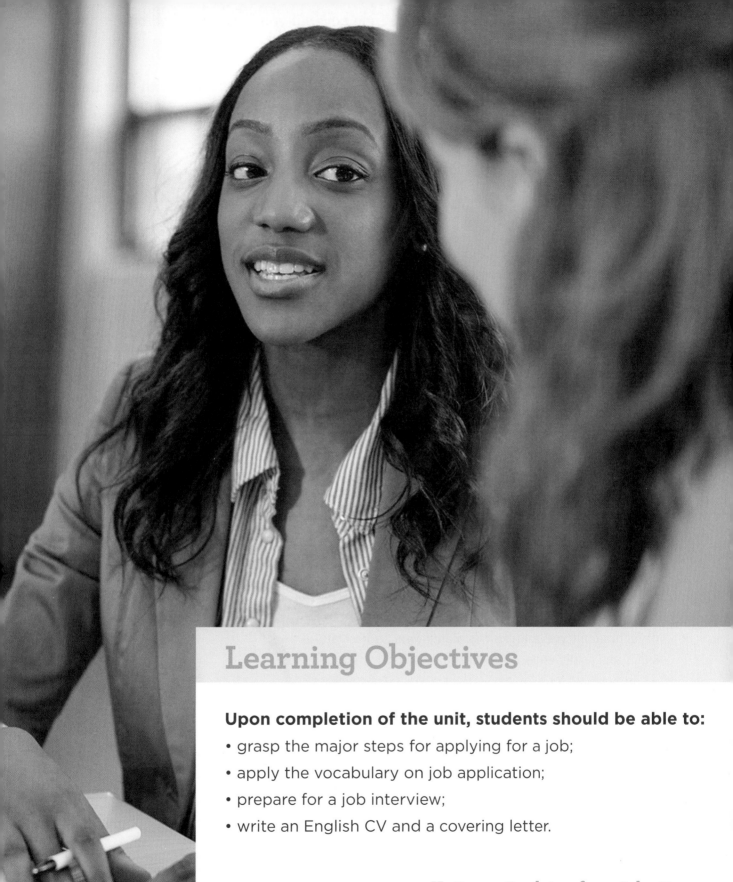

Learning Objectives

Upon completion of the unit, students should be able to:

• grasp the major steps for applying for a job;

• apply the vocabulary on job application;

• prepare for a job interview;

• write an English CV and a covering letter.

Starting Off

1 What information did your CV or resume cover, if you have prepared one?

2 Tick the things you would expect to see in a CV and discuss why with your partner.

- ☐ address
- ☐ career history
- ☐ date of birth
- ☐ favourite TV programmes

- ☐ interests
- ☐ marital status
- ☐ name
- ☐ nickname

- ☐ qualifications
- ☐ social media presence

3 Match the following hotel staff positions with their main areas of responsibility.

1) room attendant   **a** ☐ takes bookings and checks people in and out

2) concierge   **b** ☐ runs the hotel cleaning

3) desk clerk   **c** ☐ runs the hotel

4) General Manager   **d** ☐ cleans rooms and bathrooms

5) housekeeper   **e** ☐ carries luggage to and from guests' rooms

6) hotel porter   **f** ☐ assists guests by arranging tours and making bookings

Reading 1

How to write a CV

A **curriculum vitae**, CV for short, is a **brief summary** of facts about you and your **qualifications**, work history, skills and experience. It is essential to have a good CV when applying for a job as it is your chance to sell yourself and be selected for an interview. Some companies may ask you to fill in an application form instead of sending a CV. Your CV should be:

- printed on white paper and no more than 2 or 3 sides;
- clear and correct;
- **positive** and make a good impression, **emphasising** your strengths and successes;
- **adapted** to suit the specific job profile.

Key features

Personal details
Your name, address, phone number(s), email address and date of birth.

Personal profile
This is normally at the beginning of the CV. It is a short statement aimed at selling yourself so you should use positive words and expressions. It must be specifically written for the position you are applying for.

Work experience
It is normal practice to list your most recent job first, with the dates. It is not a good idea to leave any gaps between dates and if you do not have a lot of experience, you should include details of part-time and **voluntary** work.

Qualifications and training
This includes qualifications from school and university as well as any other training courses or certificates. You should **indicate** the date (the most recent first), the title of the qualification, the level obtained and the organisation/place.

Achievements/Skills/Competences
This can include foreign languages and computer skills, as well as things like artistic or musical skills. It is possible to highlight a particular **achievement** – personal or professional – which reflects well on your ability to do the job.

Interests
Hobbies or sports activities can help show particular abilities or skills which could be relevant for the job.

References
This section is for the name, position and contact details of at least two people who can provide a personal and/or work **reference**. Alternatively it is possible to state that references can be supplied on request.

MY GLOSSARY

curriculum vitae		（拉）简历	adapted	adj.	适合的
brief	adj.	简短的, 简洁的	voluntary	adj.	自愿的, 志愿的
summary	n.	总结, 概要			
qualification	n.	资格, 条件	indicate	v.	表明, 指出
positive	adj.	积极的; [数] 正的	achievement	n.	成就, 成绩; 完成
emphasise	v.	强调, 加强语气	reference	n.	参考, 参照; 参考文献

4 Read the texts and discuss these questions.

1) What is the purpose of a CV?

2) How long should it be? Why do you think that is?

3) Is it a good idea to use the same CV for different job applications? Why / Why not?

4) Why do you think the personal profile is normally at the start of the CV?

5) What order should you list your qualifications and previous jobs? Why do you think that is?

6) What kind of interests do you think would be positive to include in your CV? And negative?

7) What is the purpose of indicating references?

8) Can you think of other examples of positive words and expressions for a CV?

5 Look at the example of CV below and say whether it follows all the advice given in Reading 1.

John Clarke
hotel manager

JC

Address	7 High Street, Rochford, SS4 7PT
Phone	01702 986631
Email	john.clarke@virgin.net

Personal profile

I am highly motivated and work well as part of a team. My overseas professional experience at the Sandal's resort as a Hotel Manager taught me to adapt to new situations and to work under challenging conditions and high standard levels. I am now looking for a position as a Lodging Manager to develop my career and duties.

Qualifications

2009 – 2012 Degree in Tourism Management
Manchester University

2006 – 2008 Class BS degree in Hospitality concentration Marketing, English and French
Hope Sixth Form College, Luton

Work history

November 2012 Hotel Manager at Sandal's resort, Ocho Rios, Jamaica, WI

Sept. 2008 – June 2009 Hotel Clerk - Head of Reception - Club Med, Saint Tropez, France

Interests I enjoy scuba diving and water sports. I started sports as a team player with basketball.

References
Dr Craig Knowles
Hotel Manager at Club Med
Côte d'Azur, France

Ms Susan Knight
General Manager Sandals'
West Indies

Listening

6 **Listen to the interview between a hotel manager and a room service attendant. Complete the blanks with the missing information in the box.**

> Yes, that's not a problem for me. I prefer working at night.
>
> That's fine. I want to make a career in the hotel business.
>
> Thank you very much!
>
> It's about being polite and making sure guests have everything they need.
>
> I'm organised and efficient and I work well on my own or as part of a team.
>
> I'm a server at the Royal Hotel restaurant and I'd like some different hotel experience.

Hotel manager: OK. Tell me why you want the position of room service attendant.

Job candidate: 1) _____

Hotel manager: I see. I suppose you realise that the hours are quite long and antisocial.

Job candidate: 2) _____

Hotel manager: What skills do you think you could bring to this job?

Job candidate: 3) _____

Hotel manager: What do you understand by "customer care" in a hotel?

Job candidate: 4) _____

Hotel manager: This is an entry-level post so it offers minimum wage with gradual increases.

Job candidate: 5) _____

Hotel manager: I'll have to check your references, but if they are in order, you've got the job!

Job candidate: 6) _____

7 Listen to different members of hotel staff talking about their jobs. Decide which position each person holds.

Speaker 1 _____   Speaker 4 _____

Speaker 2 _____   Speaker 5 _____

Speaker 3 _____   Speaker 6 _____

Speaking

8 Now discuss the suitability of the candidate in Exercise 5 for the job advertised.

1) What position is being advertised?

2) What requisites are they looking for?

3) Does the candidate with the CV have the right experience and qualifications?

4) Does the CV make a positive impression? Why / Why not?

Travel Job Post - The Guardian

Job Summary

Company
Celtic Cruises

Location
London, UK

Job Type
● Full Time

Cruise Hotel Manager
About the Job

● You are responsible for the hotel operation, including coordinating and leading the Hotel Department Heads on board. You must be hands on during peak time being an example to and ensure the team delivers the product as set out in the Celtic Ocean Product: smoothly and flawlessly.

● Diploma from international recognised hotel school or university required. Min. 5 years Hotel Manager or Food & Beverage Manager on 5-star ship. Please send CV and covering letter to lewiscarol@celticruises.com

9 **Think of four tips for a successful interview and discuss them with your partner. Then, read the article below. Are they the same?**

Job interviews can be stressful; however, with the proper planning and preparation, you can get the job. Read these tips to help you survive the interview and get the job offer.

Before the interview

- Research the company and prepare relevant questions. Interviewers appreciate when job candidates show interest in the company and available position.

- Organise all paperworks, including your CV and eventual references from previous employers.

- Plan responses to common interview questions and practise interviewing with a peer.

- Prepare for questions about salary expectations by finding out how much employees in the position you are applying for are typically paid.

During the interview

- Make a good first impression by arriving on time for the interview. Make sure to dress in clean and professional attire. Finally, be polite and use the interviewer's name when speaking.

- Respond to all questions clearly. Interviewees should provide solid examples of how their previous experience relates to skills needed for the new position. Also be sure to explain your future career goals.

After the interview

- Employers may request a call-back to obtain more information as a follow-up.

10 **Make a dialogue with your partner simulating the interview. Think about what to say, how to dress and what questions to answer before the interview. After the interview, call your partner on the phone and tell him/her everything went well and thank him/her for being helpful.**

How to write a covering letter

Here you should refer to the advertisement and where you saw it. Include the title of the position and any reference number.

Here you can give a few details about your qualifications and/or experience.

This is your chance to state why you would be perfect for the company. Do not just use the same letter for every job application. Each letter should be tailored to the specific requisites mentioned in the ad.

Here you can mention any enclosures (CV, references, certificates) and state how you are going to follow up on your letter.

Colin Smith
7 High Street
Rochford
SS4 7PT
Tel: 01702 986631
colin.smith@virgin.net

17th April 20.

Ms Lewis Carol,
Celtic Cruises,
83 Wimbledon Park Side, London
SW19 5LP

Dear Ms Lewis,

I am writing in **response** to your advertisement in The Guardian and wish to apply for the post of Cruise Hotel Manager.

Since **graduating** with a first class degree in Hospitality in Luton, I have been working as a Hotel Clerk, first at Club Med as Head of Reception and then, after my degree in Tourism Management from **Manchester** University, as a Hotel Manager in Sandal's exclusive resort in **Jamaica**, where I have gained an excellent understanding of Hotel Operations.

Although I do not have any direct experience in cruise life, I have been on several cruises throughout my life, being my father a Cruise Captain.

I have always enjoyed cruises and of course working as a part of a team and I am confident that my experience of working in extreme conditions will enable me to face the demanding conditions that the position entails.

Please find enclosed my Curriculum Vitae and I would welcome the opportunity to provide further information during an interview.

I look forward to hearing from you.

Yours sincerely,

John Clarke

John Clarke

Enc.

11 Read the text and answer these questions.

1) Why is a covering letter important?

2) What are the two kinds of covering letter?

3) How should a covering letter be written?

4) How does a covering letter usually start?

5) Should a covering letter repeat all the details of a CV? Why / Why not?

6) Why is it not a good idea to use a standard covering letter for all applications?

12 Read the text again and choose the best answer.

1) What should be mentioned in the first part of a covering letter?
   A Name.   B Interests.   C Title of the position.   D References.

2) Which part should you put your qualifications in a covering letter?
   A 1st part.   B 2nd part.   C 3rd part.   D 4th part.

3) You can use the same letter in every job application.
   A True.   B False.   C Not for sure.   D Sometimes.

Writing

13 Think of a company you would like to work for and write a covering letter. Use these points for your help.

- you saw the advertisement on *The Guardian*;

- you looked at a hotel chain website;

- you are interested in the open position of lobby manager;

- you will be in London in two weeks so would be available for an interview;

- you can currently speak English and Chinese;

- you gained 3 years' experience in the same role;

- you are available in 3 months starting from today.

14 Write an English CV according to your own information. Use the words and expressions you have learnt in this unit to help you.

Photo	Name Applied Position
	Address Phone Email
Personal Profile	
Qualifications	
Work History	
Interests	
References